APPELLATE

IN THE UNITED STATES

Daniel John Meador

Jordana Simone Bernstein

ST. PAUL, MINN.
WEST PUBLISHING CO.
1994

 *TEXT IS PRINTED ON 10% POST CONSUMER RECYCLED PAPER*

 PRINTED WITH SOY INK™

CONTENTS

Appellate courts are among the most important institutions of governance in the United States. Through their review of trial court and administrative agency decisions they ensure that those bodies function lawfully and that litigants receive justice under law. Moreover, they provide authoritative interpretations of statutory and constitutional provisions and control the shaping of the common law in response to ever-changing circumstances; they are thus major sources of law. Yet, surprisingly, appellate courts are little understood, especially in light of the changes they have undergone in the last third of the twentieth century. This book is designed to assist readers—particularly American law students and jurists from other countries—in becoming better acquainted with the tribunals that play such a significant part in maintaining the rule of law.

Following the style of *American Courts* (West Publishing Co., 1991), which contains an overview of the nation's judicial systems, this book focuses specifically on the American appellate scene, consisting of more than one hundred fifty separate courts, state and federal. The book, like *American Courts*, attempts in simple, straightforward language to give both a panoramic view and many illustrative close-ups. After explaining appellate courts' purposes, it describes their authority in relation to trial courts, the various appellate structures, and the processes through which those courts bring cases to final resolution. It also provides information on the judges and other court personnel who labor to ensure that justice on appeal is done amidst an ever-rising tide of cases. Finally, the book presents ideas for enabling appellate courts to avoid engulfment and to handle their business with both efficiency and fairness. The appendices list the state and federal appellate courts in the United States and include sources that can be consulted by those interested in pursuing the subject further.

We hope that this book will not only inform its readers but will also inspire them to join in the never-ending effort to preserve and strengthen the appellate courts of this country.

DANIEL JOHN MEADOR
JORDANA SIMONE BERNSTEIN

January 1994

CHAPTER ONE

FUNCTIONS AND EVOLUTION
OF APPELLATE COURTS

A.   *What Is an Appellate Court?*

An American appellate court is a judicial body whose primary function is to review decisions made by courts subordinate to it in the judicial system or by administrative agencies. This authority is known as "appellate jurisdiction." Some appellate courts also exercise "original jurisdiction," deciding cases that have not previously been considered by other tribunals, but that is typically a small part of their business. Appellate courts are designed to be reviewing forums, devoting their attention almost entirely to deciding whether decisions of other tribunals should be affirmed, reversed, or modified in some way.

In this sense they are to be distinguished from trial courts, also known as courts of first instance. A trial court's primary mission is to take cognizance of cases when they are initiated in the judicial system, to hear testimony of witnesses and receive other evidence such as documents and things, to determine the facts of each case (often amidst a tangle of conflicting assertions), and to apply the law to those facts so as to enter judgment for one party or the other. Administrative agencies perform a similar first-instance function in cases within their authority. In contrast,

1

an appellate court typically performs no such function; it receives cases only after the trial process has run its course, in whole or in some separable part.

Appellate courts differ from trial courts in two other ways: they function collegially through units consisting of multiple judges, and they do not use juries. With rare exceptions, decisions in a trial are made either by a single judge or by a judge acting in conjunction with a jury. Juries are not involved in the appellate process because the purpose of a jury is to decide questions of fact, and appellate courts are not responsible for determining facts. Rather, they are concerned with determining whether, as a matter of law, the trial court result should be upheld or set aside. These appellate determinations are nearly always made by groups of three to nine judges, depending on the type of appellate court and the nature of the matter being decided. Although the judges in each group study and analyze each case independently, they then collegially reach a joint decision.

In deciding cases, American appellate courts consider only those facts that were determined by the judge or jury in the trial court. They rarely receive additional evidence, relying instead on the "record" made at trial, which typically consists of a typed transcript of the oral testimony (or portions of it) and the pleadings, motions, and other documents put before the trial court. Some courts use videotapes of the trial proceedings in place of typed transcripts. In addition to the record, appellate courts receive and consider arguments from counsel for the parties, either in written documents called briefs or orally in open court, or by both means.

The party who takes an appeal, *i.e.*, the one who seeks

review of a trial court decision, is generally called the "appellant," and the opposing party is called the "appellee." In cases in which a party must first obtain leave to appeal, that party is usually called the "petitioner," and the opposing party is called the "respondent."

B.   *Why Have Appellate Courts?*

Today there is a widespread and deeply held belief among American judges and lawyers that every losing litigant should have an opportunity for at least one appeal as a matter of right. Yet an appeal is not an inevitable feature of the judicial process. It is possible to construct a system in which litigation terminates in the trial court, thus achieving finality with minimal delay and expense. Indeed, the United States Constitution has not been interpreted to require either the states or the federal government to provide for an appeal in every case, and appeals have not always been available in American courts. For example, in the federal courts for many decades after their creation in the Judiciary Act of 1789, criminal convictions were not appealable at all. Civil cases could be appealed only if they involved more than $2,000, a substantial sum at that time. Why then do we now provide almost universally for appeals in all civil and criminal cases? What useful and desirable functions do appellate courts perform in American judicial systems today?

First. Appellate courts provide a means of ensuring that the law is interpreted and applied correctly and uniformly. In each state and in the federal system there are numerous trial judges—ranging from dozens in small states to hundreds in the largest states and the federal system—hearing and deciding cases individually. Even if those judges are all able and conscientious, it is inevitable that differences of view as to the content of the law will surface from time to time and that, in the hurly-burly of trials, errors will be made. It is axiomatic in our legal order that law should be applied evenhandedly and accurately to all persons within the jurisdiction. Yet correctness and uniformity in legal rulings among such a multitude of trial forums could not be afforded without a common higher court clothed with authority to review their decisions and, if necessary, reverse them. Reviewing for error is thus a large and important part of appellate work. In practice nationwide approximately ten to fifteen percent of appeals result in a reversal of the judgment below.

Second. Appellate courts provide a means for the ongoing development and evolution of the law in the common-law tradition. Legislation alone cannot deal with the multitude and variety of issues arising in litigation or keep the law evolving in a coherent way in light of changing circumstances; nor are trial courts equipped for this task. Appellate courts, through their decisions of cases and the explanations for their decisions, declare, make, and reshape legal doctrine in common-law, statutory, and constitutional fields. This aspect of their work is sometimes referred to as institutional review or lawmaking.

Error correcting and lawmaking are the core appellate functions. However, there are at least two other ends served by appellate courts.

Third. Appellate courts heighten the legitimacy and acceptability of judicial decisions. Losing litigants in the trial court are sometimes convinced that they have lost unjustifiably. Feelings that the result was unfair impair their willingness to accept it. The public likewise may think that a trial court decision was wrong and thus be reluctant to consider it a legitimate resolution of the controversy. These attitudes erode respect for law. The opportunity to take the case to a higher, multi-judge forum provides a healthy outlet for such feelings. If the appellate court affirms the judgment, the parties and the public have additional assurance that the proceeding was lawfully and properly conducted and that it was not the result of a single judge's arbitrary or idiosyncratic action. An appellate affirmance makes it clear that the judgment is that of the judiciary as an institution, acting according to established legal process.

Fourth. Appellate courts provide a means for the institutional sharing of judicial responsibility for decisions. In cases that are unusually controversial or in which the legal issues are especially difficult, judges may be uncertain about the appropriate resolution. Having the matter considered by two courts at different levels of the system and by several judges ensures that as nearly as possible the correct result is reached. The shared institutional responsibility afforded by the appellate process makes the task of judging more bearable in the close cases, especially when much is at stake and public emotions are running high and the decision is likely to be subjected to more than ordinary scrutiny and criticism. Even in run-of-the-mill cases such institutional reassurance that the system is functioning under a regime of law is valuable for the judges, as well as for the litigants and the public.

For all of these reasons, and perhaps others, appellate courts have long been considered essential features of the American judicial scene. Such courts, or similar courts, have also been long established in other countries that share the Anglo-American common-law tradition, as well as in the civil-law countries of western Europe and elsewhere. Today the view that appellate courts are essential is accepted almost universally in judicial systems around the world.

Appellate courts are also found in authoritarian regimes; they were important elements of the Marxist-Leninist systems, most of which have now been dismantled. However, it has been suggested that in such regimes appellate courts are designed not primarily to serve the interests of litigants and the rule of law but rather to provide an additional means of central control by the ruling powers, a means for transmitting commands from the top down to the grass roots.

C.   Evolution of American Appellate Structures

Since well before the beginning of the twentieth century, every American jurisdiction, state and federal, has maintained at least one distinctively appellate court, its court of last resort. Most jurisdictions now also have one or more intermediate appellate courts, which serve as reviewing tribunals located between the trial courts and the court of last resort. Today's appellate courts have judges of their own who do exclusively appellate work and rarely, if ever, participate in trial-type proceedings. But purely appellate courts and the sharp separation of trial and appellate work were not characteristic of the American judiciary in the beginning.

The early state judicial systems did not include separate reviewing courts of the modern type. Before the creation of the federal government in 1789, the judges in each state were all trial judges, sitting at various locations in the state to preside over first-instance proceedings. From time to time several of them would come together to perform an appellate function.

This style of judicial organization was inherited from the common-law courts in England. Judges of those courts would go out on circuit to sit at points around the country, acting individually as trial judges—sitting at "nisi prius," as such proceedings were called. Periodically they would convene in Westminster Hall to hear arguments on points of law that had been reserved at nisi prius and, through "writs of error," to review certain trial judge actions. The latter procedure is considered the ancestor of the modern American appeal.

In other words, there were no purely appellate judges in eighteenth-century England and America; judges were fungible, and they worked mainly at the trial level. On the eve of the ratification of the Federal Constitution, Virginia became the first state to enact legislation to establish a separate reviewing court, designated as the Court of Appeals.

In providing that the judicial power of the United States shall be vested in "one supreme Court, and in such inferior Courts" as Congress might establish, Article III of the Federal Constitution thus put forward a novel design, one not copied from any existing state judiciary. Pursuant to that constitutional authority, Congress promptly passed the Judiciary Act of 1789, creating lower courts and breathing life into the provision for a Supreme Court. Although the Supreme Court was a distinctive reviewing forum, its Justices were also required to ride circuit, presiding over trials throughout the country, thus continuing the notion of fungible judges. Indeed, in the early years the Justices spent more time at trial work than they did in their appellate role. Circuit riding remained a duty of Supreme Court Justices for over a century until Congress abolished it after the creation of separate federal courts of appeals in 1891, making the members of the Supreme Court the purely reviewing judges that they are today.

With the exceptions of Vermont and Tennessee, all states admitted to the Union after 1789 copied the federal judicial plan embodied in Article III, establishing a supreme court and a separate set of trial courts. Some of the original states continued for many decades without a separate court of last resort, having only trial judges who convened occasionally to perform appellate functions. By the early twentieth century, however, each state except Delaware had established an appellate court separate from its trial courts. Although each tier had judges of its own, in some states the judges of the top court continued to perform some trial duties until the beginning of the twentieth century.

Since the emergence of separate courts of last resort, the most significant structural change in many American judicial systems has been the introduction of intermediate appellate courts. The creation of such a court divides the appellate structure into two levels. These two-level appellate structures, and the functions of each level, are discussed in Chapter 2.

D. The Contemporary Appellate Scene

The appellate courts in American judicial systems go by a variety of names. (See Appendices A, B, and C.) The court at the apex of each system, the court of last resort, is usually called the "Supreme Court," and that is the term that will be used in this book. However, in Maryland and New York it is called the Court of Appeals, and there are variations in a few other states. The intermediate appellate courts that exist in thirty-eight states and the federal system most frequently bear the name "Court of Appeals," but several states use other names. These bodies will be referred to in this book as intermediate courts.

Judges who serve on a court denominated "Supreme Court" usually carry the official title of Justice. The presiding officer is the Chief Justice. For those sitting on a tribunal named "Court of Appeals" the usual title is Judge. The presiding officer is the Chief Judge. All of these judicial officials, regardless of the type of court on which they serve, will be generically referred to hereafter as judges.

Supreme courts in some states are housed in the state capitol, along with the legislative chambers and executive offices. In other states, the court inhabits its own building; some of these judicial buildings date back to the nineteenth century, while others are late twentieth-century structures. The United States Supreme Court occupies its own impressive marble building completed in 1935, just east of the Capitol in Washington. Intermediate courts are housed in a wide variety of buildings. Some are in the state's judicial building along with the supreme court. Others occupy buildings of their own, while some are quartered in nondescript office buildings.

The courtroom of a court of last resort is typically a high-ceilinged, ornate space, often with marble walls or columns and rich-textured draperies and carpeting. Across the front is a massive shoulder-high mahogany bench behind which the judges sit in a row of tall, leather upholstered chairs. A little way in front of the bench is a podium from which lawyers address the court, flanked by large tables at which the lawyers sit during the argument of their case when it is not their turn at the podium. To the rear of the tables is a low wooden railing known as the bar, and behind the bar there are usually several rows of pew-like seats for the public.

The bench, the robes worn by the judges, and the general ambience are all descended from the common-law courts sitting in Westminster Hall over two centuries ago. A similar ambience and setting can be found today in the Royal Courts of Justice in London and in appellate courts around the world in those countries that stand in the common-law tradition. In the United States, these quiet, dignified courtrooms symbolize, as perhaps no other physical space does, the concept of government under law, a concept whose vitality depends in no small measure on courts, and ultimately on appellate courts, to determine what the law is and, if necessary, to hold that even government itself has acted illegally.

The judges' individual chambers are often located along the corridors to the rear and sides of the courtroom, shut off from the public. Each set of chambers typically includes a large room for the judge, a room for the secretary, and one or more rooms for the law clerks. Shelves filled with law books line the walls; in addition the courthouse usually contains an extensive law library, which is available also to the public. The court's private conference room is typically located in the vicinity of the judges' chambers; it features a large table around which the judges sit to discuss and decide cases.

In some intermediate courts the physical arrangements are similar to those in state supreme courts, but courtrooms and judges' chambers are usually smaller and less ornate. Some large, busy courts have several courtrooms, making it possible for oral arguments to be heard simultaneously by different panels of the court.

Compared with trial courts, appellate courts are relatively invisible. Although the court clerk's office is open to the public every business day to receive papers and dispense information, the judges can be seen only a few days a month when they sit behind the massive bench in the courtroom to hear oral arguments. From three to six cases will typically be set for argument on each of those days. The lawyers for the parties will be present, but there will usually be only a handful of spectators, if any. The proceeding tends to be quiet and formal, although there are sometimes lively interchanges between judges and counsel. These hearings in open court play a relatively small part today in the appellate process, which is, rather, a process heavily dependent on written material.

The contrast with a trial court is striking. There, one will find courtrooms in constant use amidst a great deal of hustle and bustle, with jurors in the box, witnesses being interrogated, lawyers animatedly making objections and motions, and often numerous spectators coming and going. A trial judge is daily involved in a highly public proceeding, whereas appellate judges lead a rather monastic life, cloistered in their chambers with briefs, records, law books, a secretary or two, and from one to four law clerks. They often do not even see their judicial colleagues except on the few days monthly when they gather to hear oral arguments and perhaps at a monthly conference to discuss pending cases.

On most days a visitor can wander through the precincts of an appellate court and encounter a deserted courtroom, empty corridors, and no human beings other than the personnel in the clerk's office. A museum-like appearance may be imparted by the presence along the walls of life-size portraits of bygone judges, all black-robed and somber, oracles of the law from earlier eras. To outsiders there is little or no indication that behind closed doors in other parts of the building, judges and their assistants are laboring mightily to maintain the rule of law under the extraordinarily heavy caseloads that now afflict many American appellate courts.

E.   *Late Twentieth-Century Appellate Growth*

Beginning in the 1960s, the volume of appeals in American appellate courts began to rise. The growth was uneven and was much greater in some jurisdictions than in others. However, there was some degree of increase everywhere. The increases continued year after year and began in some places to accelerate to such a level that appellate courts were said to be facing a "crisis of volume."

Since then, the crisis has worsened. The federal system has seen the most appellate growth; annual filings in the United States Courts of Appeals nationwide rose from 3,899 in 1960 to 47,013 in 1992. The increases in many states have also been substantial. Between 1952 and 1982, several states experienced growth in appellate filings in excess of 1,000% (*e.g.*, Arizona, Maryland, Oregon); others saw a six- or sevenfold increase (*e.g.*, New Jersey, Virginia, Washington). The increases continue unabated. For example, California, having experienced a fivefold growth in appeals in the twenty years before 1982, saw appeals rise from more than 15,000 in that year to more than 21,000 in 1992. Although at times in the past appeals have gone through periods of growth, the degree of growth in the last third of the twentieth century is unprecedented.

Not all of the causes for this growth can be determined, but some contributing factors can be identified. Criminal appeals have shot up most markedly, as a result of the provision of free legal counsel and of other measures that make free appeals available to convicted indigents. Moreover, defendants now can contest more matters as a result of Supreme Court decisions expanding their rights under the U.S. Constitution. The causes of the increase in civil appeals are more difficult to identify. One cause is the general rise in civil litigation at the trial level, attributed to factors such as the growing heterogeneity of American society, increasing urbanization, and the erosion of institutions such as the family, the church, and other organizations that formerly worked to resolve many disputes. Although more trial court litigation naturally results in more appeals, the growth in appeals has been proportionately far greater than the growth in litigation generally. In the federal courts, for example, appeals increased tenfold over the past thirty years, while trial business grew only threefold. Whatever the reasons, litigants seem less willing than before to rest content with trial court decisions.

The high and constantly growing volume of appeals is the dominant concern in American appellate life in the late twentieth century. It affects all else in the appellate realm. Steps in response to volume taken by appellate judges and by legislatures have wrought substantial changes in the appellate courts. Those judicial institutions today are in significant ways different from what they were in 1960, although their role and functions in the legal order remain essentially what they have always been.

Much of the remainder of this book focuses on the changes made in an effort to keep abreast of the appellate workload and avoid inundation. Chapter 2 deals with structural alterations in response to volume. Following Chapter 3's discussion of the rules governing access to appellate courts, Chapter 4 describes traditional appellate procedure and late twentieth-century modifications in internal decisional processes. Chapter 5 deals with appellate judges and with personnel changes in response to the growth in volume. The extent to which these developments collectively have impaired the quality of the appellate process and fundamentally altered the nature of appellate courts is one of the most challenging questions of our time. An equally challenging question, addressed in Chapter 6, is whether—and what—other measures can be adopted to enable appellate courts to adjudicate what appears to be a never-ending rise in the number of appeals.

CHAPTER TWO

STRUCTURE AND ORGANIZATION
OF APPELLATE COURTS

A. *One-Level and Two-Level Appellate Structures*

There are fifty-three independent American judicial systems, each with its own court of last resort: the fifty states, the District of Columbia, the Commonwealth of Puerto Rico, and the federal system. The supreme courts in these systems range in size from five to nine judges each. A majority have seven members, including those in some of the largest states. The United States Supreme Court and a few of the state supreme courts have nine. (See Appendix A.)

A curious departure from the national pattern of a single supreme court exists in Texas and Oklahoma. Each of those states maintains two courts of last resort: one for civil cases (the supreme court) and one for criminal cases (the court of criminal appeals). Both supreme courts have nine judges. The criminal appeals court in Texas also has nine judges; the one in Oklahoma has five.

The view is widely held among American judges and lawyers that a court of last resort should have at least five but no more than nine judges. This position is taken in the American Bar Association's *Standards of Judicial Administration*, a comprehensive statement of the features of court structure and process deemed optimal by the nation's largest organization of lawyers and judges. Five is thought to be the minimum number needed to provide an appropriate balance of perspectives and judicial judgments for a tribunal that is authoritatively enunciating the law of an entire jurisdiction; nine is considered the maximum number that can participate meaningfully in a genuinely collegial decision. This attitude about size is based on the belief that a court of last resort should always sit en banc (all of its judges sitting together) when deciding a case on the merits (as distinguished, *e.g.*, from deciding whether to grant review as a matter of discretion or acting on a purely procedural issue).

Consistency of legal doctrine and efficiency in the appellate process can be best achieved in a judicial system that has only one appellate court. In such a structure, all appeals go from the trial courts to the one appellate forum. Only one review of any case is possible, and there is no confusion over jurisdictional lines, no question about which appeals go where. Because all appeals are decided by one court, there is no possibility of conflicting decisions between courts; the likelihood of maintaining system-wide uniformity in decisional law is thus at its maximum.

A single supreme court sitting en banc in all cases works well, however, only as long as the volume of appeals does not exceed the capacity of that court. In the first half of the twentieth century, as the rising quantity of appeals began to overload some state supreme courts, those courts began to sit in panels. For example, a court of seven members would divide the caseload between two four-judge panels (with the chief justice serving as the fourth member of each panel). If a panel decision were unanimous, that was the final decision of the court. If there were a dissent, the case would be referred to the full court for decision. Sitting in panels enabled the court to decide many more cases annually than it could have decided by always sitting en banc.

Another means employed by state supreme courts to keep abreast of the rising tide of appeals was to enlist the assistance of "commissioners," lawyers appointed by the court to hear arguments in appeals and write drafts of opinions. The judges would review the drafts and, if they agreed, would adopt them as opinions of the court. This professional assistance made it possible for the court to increase substantially its output of decisions. State supreme court use of such commissioners reached its high point shortly before the Second World War; in the post-war years this type of judicial officer disappeared.

Both of these devices—sitting in panels and using commissioners—came to be regarded as temporary expedients. They were never ideal or desirable, and they provided no long-range solution to the ever-growing volume of appeals. The idea of adding judges to the court was often discussed but was not adopted because of the conviction that the top court should function as a single unit and that this could not be done with more than nine judges. Instead, the long-term solution, structural in nature and now widely employed, was the insertion of a new judicial tier between the supreme court and the trial courts. This step serves two objectives: it relieves the overload on the top court, and it increases the system's total appellate capacity.

The federal intermediate tier was created in 1891. The first judicial system to take this step was that of Ohio, which established an intermediate appellate court in 1883. Other states followed suit in the years thereafter, and by 1911 there were intermediate appellate courts in sixteen states, although three states later discontinued them. Several decades were to pass before this innovation spread to other states. By the late 1950s there were still only thirteen states with intermediate courts. In 1957, on the eve of the late twentieth-century appellate upsurge, Florida became the next state to establish an intermediate tier.

With the rapid rise of appeals beginning in the 1960s, the idea spread, and by 1991 thirty-eight states had established bi-level appellate structures. (See Appendix B.) Those states and the federal system have what is usually described as a three-tiered judicial system; the bottom tier is the broad base of trial courts, the middle tier the intermediate appellate court or courts, and the top tier—the apex of the judicial pyramid—the supreme court.

B.   Organization of the Intermediate Appellate Level

The intermediate judicial tier, located between the trial courts and the court of last resort, can be organized in one of three ways: by establishing a single, jurisdiction-wide court (the single-court design); by establishing two or more co-equal courts in different geographical areas within the jurisdiction (the geographical design); or by establishing two or more co-equal courts with authority over different categories of cases (the subject-matter design). Each has advantages and disadvantages.

The Single-Court Design. A majority of the states with three-tiered judicial systems (but not the federal judiciary) maintain only one intermediate court. That tribunal hears appeals from trial courts throughout the state. If the volume of appeals is sufficiently low, the court can sit en banc on every appeal. However, this is usually not the case, so most of the statewide intermediate courts function through rotating three-judge panels. Functioning through panels is deemed acceptable in an intermediate court because such a court, unlike a court of last resort, is not responsible for the definitive enunciation of the state's law.

A court that sits in panels can consist of as many judges as are necessary to deal with the volume of business. Statewide appellate courts usually have from six to a dozen judges. A few have substantially more; the largest are the New Jersey Appellate Division with twenty-eight and the Michigan Court of Appeals with twenty-four. A few have only three.

The two major advantages of this style of organization are efficiency and doctrinal coherence. Efficiency is fostered because the appellate business of the state can be centrally managed and the work distributed evenly among the judges. Three-judge panels can sit anywhere in the state, in accordance with appellate demands, or the court can always sit at one convenient location, whichever arrangement better suits the needs of the day. Having a single set of statewide appellate procedural rules facilitates the task of lawyers whose practice spans different parts of the state.

Doctrinal coherence is promoted because it is easier to avoid inconsistencies in decisions and to maintain uniformity in the law when all of the judges in the intermediate tier are under one management. Internal procedures can be devised to foster consistency in a way that would not be possible with separate courts. Moreover, collegiality can be heightened and the likelihood of decisional harmony increased when all of the state's intermediate appellate judges associate together on the same court.

The single-court form of organization becomes less workable as the territory and population of the jurisdiction increase. Large, populous jurisdictions tend to adopt a dispersed, geographical plan of intermediate appellate organization.

The Geographical Design. Under this scheme, the jurisdiction is divided territorially into regions usually designated as numbered judicial districts or circuits (or sometimes as named divisions), and an appellate court is established in each. Nine states and the federal system have adopted this plan.

In the states with this regional plan of appellate organization, the number of intermediate courts ranges from two in Arizona to twelve in Ohio and fourteen in Texas. The other states have from three to six intermediate courts. The number of judges on each regional court ranges from three to a dozen or more. They typically sit in three-judge panels. Each of these courts has authority over appeals from the trial courts located in its territorial region. In a few states with a single statewide intermediate court, designated three-judge panels sit regularly in particular regions (*e.g.*, Oklahoma, Washington, Wisconsin), thus approaching a de facto geographical design.

In the federal system, spanning the entire United States, there are twelve geographical circuits. Eleven are denominated numerically as the First through the Eleventh; the other is the District of Columbia Circuit. In each circuit there is a United States Court of Appeals. These courts range in size from six judges in the First Circuit to twenty-eight in the Ninth. They regularly function through rotating three-judge panels, though they have authority to sit en banc. Each circuit court hears appeals from the federal trial courts (called district courts) located in its circuit and also entertains appeals from certain federal administrative agencies. Each of these courts has its headquarters at a central location, but panels often sit in other places within the circuit.

The federal circuits vary greatly in their territorial expanse. Among the numbered circuits, the smallest is the First, which covers Maine, New Hampshire, Massachusetts, Rhode Island, and Puerto Rico, and the largest is the Ninth, which embraces seven far western states plus Alaska, Hawaii, and other Pacific islands. The District of Columbia Circuit includes only the District. (See Appendix C.)

The advantages of the geographical arrangement are that it makes the appellate courts more conveniently accessible to lawyers and litigants throughout a large territorial area and takes into account varying regional interests by having a forum whose judges are drawn from the region. Geographical organization may also facilitate case management where the totality of appellate business throughout the jurisdiction might overwhelm a single intermediate court. A disadvantage of this arrangement is that it creates the possibility for inconsistencies in the decisional law, with one regional court deciding an issue differently from the way it is decided in another regional court. The maintenance of doctrinal consistency within the intermediate tier is discussed below in Section D.

The Subject-Matter Design. Under both the single-court and geographical designs the traditional practice is that each court and all panels on it may hear and decide appeals of all kinds, spanning the entire corpus of the law. In contrast, under the subject-matter plan, an appellate court or panel is allotted only a portion of the appellate business, defined by types of cases; its jurisdiction over those cases is exclusive of all other appellate courts or panels (except the court of last resort sitting above it). This scheme of appellate organization has been developed to a high degree in Germany, and it is also found in other countries that follow the civil-law tradition.

The best American example of subject-matter organization is the United States Court of Appeals for the Federal Circuit, established by Congress in 1982. The court is headquartered in Washington, D.C., and is coequal with the twelve geographically organized federal intermediate appellate courts, but its authority, unlike that of the regional courts, is not confined territorially. Rather, it is nationwide in scope and is defined by the subject matter of the cases or by the origin of the appeals. The Federal Circuit has jurisdiction over appeals from federal district courts throughout the country in patent cases and in certain suits to recover damages from the government. In addition, it has jurisdiction over all appeals from certain other forums, including the Court of International Trade, the Court of Federal Claims, the Merit Systems Protection Board, and some administrative agencies. Even though it does not hear appeals spanning the entire range of legal issues, its jurisdiction is still quite varied.

The subject-matter plan of appellate organization has not gained wide popularity in the states. It can be found in Pennsylvania, where the Commonwealth Court has jurisdiction over appeals in cases involving local government units and from state administrative agencies, while the Superior Court takes appeals in all other civil cases and in criminal cases. Alabama and Tennessee maintain separate intermediate courts for civil and criminal cases. As previously mentioned, Texas and Oklahoma have separate civil and criminal courts of last resort.

Subject-matter courts are inconsistent with the American

Bar Association's standards on court organization, which assert that every appellate court should have jurisdiction over the entire range of appellate business. Many lawyers and judges agree with that view. Their apprehension about subject-matter organization seems to stem from their confusing it with specialization.

A subject-matter court need not be specialized. Appellate specialization occurs if a court entertains appeals in only one relatively narrow category of case. For example, a court could properly be called specialized if its jurisdiction were restricted to deciding patent appeals or workers' compensation cases. The illustration most often cited in the federal system, usually with horror, is the Commerce Court, which existed for a few years just before the First World War. Its jurisdiction was confined to reviewing orders of the Interstate Commerce Commission. It exhibited, or at least suggested to observers, the dangers thought to accompany specialization: risk of capture by those with special interests in the court's work (there, the railroads), tendencies of the judges to lose contact with the general body of jurisprudence and develop esoteric legal views, and difficulty in attracting able lawyers to the bench. However, the U.S. Court of Appeals for the Federal Circuit shows that those dangers can be avoided while at the same time designated categories of cases are routed to a single court; the key to success is the variety of business given the court.

An appellate court with a caseload consisting solely of criminal matters is generally disfavored in the American legal world. In addition to some of the reasons against specialization just mentioned, it is thought that because of the peculiar human element in criminal matters and their special social importance, it is preferable to have criminal appeals decided by a court with at least some judges who also decide appeals in other legal fields.

Thus the scheme found in Texas, Oklahoma, Alabama, and Tennessee does not enjoy wide acceptance.

The subject-matter style of appellate organization has several advantages. It avoids conflicting decisions on the same legal issue—one of the major problems of co-equal regional courts—because only one court decides any given type of case. It also provides the optimum means of achieving coherent development of legal doctrine; a given group of judges dealing over time with a body of law within its exclusive jurisdiction develops a knowledge of the subject and its nuances that judges dealing only occasionally with the issues cannot attain. This familiarity enhances efficiency and productivity because the judges do not need to re-educate themselves each time a particular legal issue comes before them. Continuity of decision makers also helps lawyers to predict the likely outcome of appeals and thus retards the filing of hopeless ones.

The only disadvantages of subject-matter organization in the intermediate tier are encountered if a court's jurisdiction is defined too narrowly, thus making it a specialized court. The dangers of specialization can be avoided by giving the court authority over a varied array of case types.

C.   *Relationships Between the Two Appellate Levels*

When a judicial structure is expanded vertically by inserting an intermediate appellate tier—whether of the single-court, geographical, or subject-matter variety—it is necessary to decide how the appellate functions are to be allocated. The two appellate levels will be sharing the work formerly done by one. A legislature creating such a bifurcated structure must decide which level will do what and should design procedures to ensure that the functions of each level are performed without unnecessary delay and duplication.

An intermediate court is in an odd position. It looks in two directions simultaneously—down to the trial courts and up to the court of last resort. It is clothed with authority to reverse the trial courts, but it in turn can be reversed by the top court. Its insertion into the judicial pyramid creates a potential for complications, added expense to litigants, and delay in the ultimate resolution of controversies. The challenge for judicial architects is to fit the new tier into the existing pyramid in a way that maximizes its potential advantages while avoiding its possible dysfunctional effects. Below we sketch the array of jurisdictional and procedural arrangements that can be employed to fit the middle tier into the judicial structure.

Discretionary Second Review in the Court of Last Resort

While it is widely believed that every losing litigant should have the opportunity as a matter of right to a review, it is also believed that one review is sufficient to protect a litigant's interest in an error-free trial proceeding. Two reviews, absent special justification in a particular case, are seen as wasteful of judicial resources, imposing undue expense on litigants, and unnecessary to protect the rights of the parties.

The specter of double appeals has always haunted the creation of intermediate appellate courts. As a result, in three-tiered judicial systems it is generally provided that an appeal may be taken as a matter of right to the intermediate court but that any further review in the supreme court is at the discretion of that court. Thus double appeals can occur only with the top court's permission. This is the arrangement in the federal system and in many state systems.

Under that arrangement the top court is freed from reviewing the mass of appeals and can therefore devote its energies to deciding cases of significance to the legal order and the public interest. The intermediate court is a buffer, a breakwater against which the tidal waves of appeals spend themselves, leaving the top court protected in quieter waters to deliberate on specially important questions. Another way of putting the matter is to say that the supreme court is concerned primarily with the development of the law, while the intermediate court is concerned primarily with the application of existing law.

This division of responsibility rests on the premise that all appellate work can be sorted into the two categories of error correcting and lawmaking (or law declaring, as some prefer), discussed in Chapter 1. In performing its lawmaking responsibility, also known as institutional review, a supreme court chooses the cases it will consider and decide from among the petitions filed with it. Error correcting is assigned to intermediate courts, which receive appeals directly from the trial courts and typically have no discretion to decline to decide any case.

It is assumed that a court reviewing for correctness applies established rules of law to determine whether the trial court committed error. But the function of error correction is not always neatly separable from that of lawmaking. The task of deciding cases inevitably involves some measure of law declaring, as the appellate court must articulate the legal precept being applied even when that precept has not previously been articulated in precisely the same way. In the course of applying established rules to varying factual situations, the intermediate court may at times unavoidably affect the development of the law. Moreover, in cases of first impression, for which there is no established rule, the court must formulate one. However, the intermediate court does not have the last say if review in the supreme court is sought and granted. In practice, though, the finite capacity of a court of last resort prevents its reviewing more than a small percentage of intermediate court decisions, thus leaving the latter as the final ruling in a great many cases.

Although some lawmaking by the intermediate court is inescapable, that court must follow the law as enunciated by its court of last resort. Its primary mission is to apply the existing law of the jurisdiction as best it can interpret it, not to make new law. Invoking that principle in a 1973 opinion, the Florida Supreme Court chastised one of the state's intermediate courts for holding that the doctrine of contributory negligence would no longer be followed and that the doctrine of comparative negligence would replace it, saying that only the supreme court could make such a change. Yet the court then proceeded in that same opinion to reach the identical result that the intermediate court had reached, thus evidencing that the latter's view of Florida law had been correct. The point being made, however, was that it was for the supreme court, not the intermediate court, to say so.

Sometimes language or trends in the supreme court's opinions, particularly if accompanied by a recent, significant change in its membership, reveal that a prior decision would no longer be adhered to. In such situations some intermediate courts have not considered themselves bound by the prior decision, on the reasoning that it no longer represented the law of the jurisdiction. To take such a position, however, risks introducing uncertainty into the law, and most intermediate appellate judges would probably say (as would trial judges) that supreme court decisions, even though thought to be unsound, outmoded, and doomed to oblivion, must be followed until overruled by the supreme court itself.

An intermediate court can, of course, write an opinion criticizing an existing common-law rule and suggesting that it be modified or abandoned for reasons stated. Such a step calls the problem to the attention of the top court and the legislature, either of which can appropriately address the matter. In this way intermediate courts can make useful contributions to the development of legal doctrine even though they lack definitive authority in that regard.

The supreme court's discretion to review or not review an intermediate court's decision is typically unlimited by statute or constitution. However, top courts with that sort of discretionary jurisdiction—usually referred to as "certiorari jurisdiction"—have adopted rules that in varying degrees of particularity describe the situations in which the court is likely to take a case. The situations listed in these rules often include the following: when the intermediate court's decision conflicts with a decision of another intermediate court or conflicts with a decision of the supreme court, when the case involves an issue of law that has not been but should be authoritatively resolved, and when the court below has so far departed from the normal course of judicial procedure as to call for an exercise of the top court's supervisory authority. The U.S. Supreme Court has a rule of this sort, and it has served as a model for many of the state supreme courts' rules.

This kind of rule serves the purpose of letting the bar and the public know that the court does not exercise its discretion idiosyncratically or arbitrarily, but rather acts in accordance with some rational criteria. It also gives guidance to lawyers as to the kinds of cases the court is interested in reviewing, thus working to discourage hopeless petitions. In addition, the rule provides a structure for the judges themselves, some standards under which they can discuss petitions and perhaps achieve a more consistent pattern of grants and denials. These rules, however, usually contain a good deal of general language so that they do not operate to restrain the judges unduly.

Double Appeals as a Matter of Right

Because of the widely accepted view that a second appeal should be permitted only in the interest of the legal system, and then only in the discretion of the court of last resort, double appeals as a matter of right are rare. They are not authorized in the federal system or in most states. One of the few states with such a procedure is Ohio. There an intermediate court decision affirming a death sentence or deciding a state or federal constitutional question can be appealed to the supreme court, which is bound to review the case on its merits.

The interests sought to be protected by such a duplicating review can be protected as well or better by providing one or more of the procedures described below, while avoiding the expense, delay, and drain on judicial resources caused by giving parties the right to two appeals.

By-pass and Short-stop

The possibility of double review can be eliminated altogether by devices referred to as "by-pass" and "short-stop." These devices operate to limit the parties to a single review by foreclosing one or the other of the appellate levels.

A by-pass procedure routes appeals directly from the trial courts to the supreme court, thus avoiding the intermediate tier completely. In every three-tiered system there are provisions for at least a few by-passes. These are specified by statute and typically include types of cases that are deemed to be of sufficient importance that they should or likely will go to the supreme court in any event; time and expense are thus saved by routing them there from the outset. Often included in such statutes are criminal cases in which the death sentence has been imposed and cases in which the trial court has held a statute unconstitutional. In some states only a handful of by-passes are authorized, while in others the by-pass provisions are extensive. The more extensive the array of by-passes, the more the supreme court performs an error-correcting function, thus assuming the role of the intermediate court, in addition to its institutional role.

The only by-pass in the federal system is for decisions of three-judge district courts (convened by statute, mainly in cases challenging the constitutionality of legislative apportionment); appeals in those cases go directly to the Supreme Court.

The short-stop operates to terminate cases in the intermediate court by prohibiting further review. The theory is that for certain types of cases the interests of the legal order can be served sufficiently by review at the intermediate level and that the costs and delay of a second review, or even the effort to secure a second review, are not justified. The intermediate court is thus left in charge of monitoring and developing the decisional law in those areas, in addition to performing its error-correcting function.

Examples of short-stop provisions can be found in several states. They include workers' compensation cases, cases in which the only issue is the sufficiency of the evidence, and cases in which the intermediate court has affirmed the denial of a motion to dismiss, the denial of a motion for judgment on the pleadings, or the denial of a motion for summary judgment. In Virginia, which has employed the short-stop device more extensively than most other states, cases that terminate with the intermediate court's decision include traffic infractions, misdemeanors for which no incarceration has been imposed, cases originating before administrative agencies, and domestic relations cases.

Some short-stop statutes do not absolutely bar further review in the supreme court; the door is left ajar for constitutional questions. Apart from that exception, the effect of the short-stop, in the specified cases, is to leave the intermediate court as the court of last resort.

We turn now to a variety of provisions among the federal and state systems for moving cases between the two appellate levels once an appeal has been taken. No system employs all of these; they appear in various combinations.

Leap-frog

Where a "leap-frog" procedure is authorized, once an appeal has been taken to the intermediate court either party can immediately petition the supreme court for review without awaiting a decision at the intermediate level. This procedure permits cases of great urgency and importance to move to the supreme court without the delay that would be involved in first obtaining a decision from the intermediate court.

Federal law contains such a provision. Instances in which it has been used include the steel seizure case (challenge to President's seizure of steel mills), the Pentagon papers case (effort to prevent publication of government documents concerning the Vietnam War), and the Nixon tapes case (President's challenge to subpoena). The Supreme Court's leap-frog jurisdiction is discretionary, and the Court has stressed that it will use this authority sparingly.

Leap-frogging's advantage is that it makes possible a greatly accelerated resolution of the controversy. Its disadvantage is that the supreme court is deprived of the benefit of the intermediate judges' views to aid it in its decision.

Certification

Under a certification procedure, an intermediate court itself can send a case to the supreme court. Provisions of this sort are found in many states and in the federal system. Some provide that the intermediate court may certify the entire case, thus passing total decisional authority to the supreme court, while others also provide for certification of specific issues. In the latter instance, the intermediate court retains the case on its docket to await receipt of the top court's answer, after which it proceeds to a disposition of the appeal in light of the answer.

The idea behind this procedure is that when the intermediate court believes that a case or an issue is one that should be decided by the supreme court, and that it would probably go on up in any event, time and money are saved by sending it there without pausing to decide it. This sort of certification is in the discretion of the intermediate court. Some supreme courts also have a discretion to decline to entertain the certified matter, thus forcing the intermediate court to decide it.

Reach-down

Under leap-frog and certification procedures, cases reach the court of last resort through actions of the parties and the intermediate court respectively. In contrast, under a "reach-down" procedure the top court is empowered on its own initiative to pluck a case up from the intermediate court for final decision. Many states have reach-down statutes; the federal system does not.

There are two situations in which such an authority in the top court could be useful. One is when the intermediate court is backlogged, with the prospect of inordinate delays in getting the accumulated appeals decided. The supreme court can relieve the congestion by reaching down and taking up for decision a large quantity of the appeals awaiting consideration, thus serving the interests of the parties in an earlier resolution of their disputes and also aiding the intermediate court in catching up with its caseload.

The other situation in which the reach-down procedure can be useful is when an unusually important case is pending in the intermediate court, one as to which there is urgent public need for a prompt, definitive decision. If the parties have not taken steps to invoke the supreme court's jurisdiction and the intermediate court has not certified the case, the supreme court, under a reach-down provision, can act on its own to bring the case up. It is not clear, however, how the supreme court officially would learn of the pendency of the case in this circumstance.

Reference (or Pour-over)

In several states the appellate business is allocated between the two levels through a case-by-case determination by the supreme court. Examples are Hawaii, Idaho, and Iowa. All appeals are taken initially from the trial courts to the supreme court. Through an internal screening procedure, that court then sends some cases to the intermediate court and retains others for itself. Under this "reference" or "pour-over" jurisdiction, the intermediate court receives its cases solely from the top court. The supreme court's routing decision is generally based on the distinction between error correcting and law declaring. Cases seen as involving only the former are sent to the intermediate court, while those involving the latter are retained.

Reference or pour-over statutes usually provide that after a decision of a referred case in the intermediate court a party may petition the supreme court for discretionary review. However, if that court's initial screening has been done well, review will rarely be desirable or necessary.

An advantage of this jurisdictional arrangement is that it allows for a more refined allocation of appellate business between the two levels than can be achieved through a general statute that must by necessity speak in terms of categories of cases, resulting in some cases going initially to the intermediate court when they should have gone straight to the top court. Also, it permits the supreme court to manage efficiently the totality of the state's appellate business by allocating cases to the less backlogged of the two appellate courts. A disadvantage is that the screening process occupies some of the supreme court justices' time and effort that might better be put into deciding important cases. That problem can be met, however, at least to some extent, by the use of central staff attorneys, assistants whose work is discussed in Chapter 5.

In the federal judicial system there is no reference or pour-over jurisdiction. The idea was much discussed, however, during the 1970s and 1980s in connection with proposals for the creation of a national court of appeals or an inter-circuit tribunal. This subject is treated further in Chapter 6.

D.   Maintaining Doctrinal Coherence Within the Intermediate Level

Although the court of last resort in a three-tiered judicial system has ultimate responsibility for maintaining uniformity and coherence in legal doctrine, it is desirable that within the intermediate tier the law be interpreted and applied as harmoniously as possible. The judicial system at all levels should strive to speak with a consistent voice and to treat litigants evenhandedly. Maintaining internal uniformity of decisions within the intermediate level is especially important if the volume of litigation is so large that the top court cannot, as a practical matter, review more than a small percentage of the intermediate decisions. That is in fact the situation today in the federal system and some states. In that circumstance, the intermediate courts must to a high degree look to themselves to keep their own legal house in order. Doing this, however, has become increasingly difficult as the volume of appeals has grown. Indeed, the intermediate courts, created to relieve problems of volume in top courts, have themselves now become the locus of those problems.

A single jurisdiction-wide intermediate court of relatively small size (no more than nine judges) can achieve uniformity with little difficulty. If the court regularly sits en banc, as a court of that size can do if the quantity of appeals is not too great, there is no problem; the court is functioning as a single decisional unit, the optimum arrangement in the interest of doctrinal harmony. Even if such a court sits in rotating three-judge panels, the threat to coherence is relatively small. The judges are few enough so that each will frequently sit with all the others, and they are apt to develop a considerable measure of collegiality. They can keep abreast of all panel opinions and thus be familiar with the entire range of the court's jurisprudence. As a further precaution against decisional disharmony, draft opinions can be circulated to all of the court's judges for comment prior to issuance.

If, however, the intermediate court sits in fixed panels, the risk of inconsistency rises. A court of nine judges, for example, working in three-judge, non-rotating panels whose members remain together over lengthy periods of time, could tend to become in effect three separate tribunals, each focused on its own work with little attention paid to the decisions of other panels. Thus, if panels on an intermediate court are randomly assigned appeals from all across the court's docket, doctrinal harmony is best promoted by regular rotation of panel composition, and this is the prevailing pattern in state and federal judicial systems.

The difficulty of maintaining consistency in decisional law increases markedly when the intermediate tier is organized on a geographical basis, with two or more co-equal regional courts each deciding appeals of all types from within its territory. As mentioned earlier, that is the appellate structure in the federal system and in nine states. The general view is that no one such court is bound to follow the decisions of any other such court within its system; these are independent appellate tribunals,

subject only to the reviewing power of their common court of last
resort. Although one regional court will usually accord respect to
the decisions of another, these courts are not reluctant to reach
decisions on legal questions different from those reached on the
same questions by their companion courts. As a result conflicting
pronouncements on legal doctrine are inevitable from time to
time. The only means of eliminating those conflicts, given this
type of appellate organization, is review by the top court.

That arrangement works relatively well if the top court is
able to grant review in all instances of conflicting intermediate
court decisions. However, as indicated above, the ever-increasing
growth of appeals in the late twentieth century has outrun the
capacity of the supreme court in some large jurisdictions, with the
result that some conflicts go unresolved or at least remain
unresolved for a long while. In the view of many observers this
condition now exists in the federal system, although the number
and nature of inter-circuit conflicts is a matter of debate.

A double threat of decisional disharmony exists if the
regional courts are organized internally into three-judge panels.
There is then the possibility of inconsistency not only between the
separate regional courts but also within each regional court. The
internal threat is small if the judges are few in number, but if
they are numerous a significant problem can arise. The risk of
intra-court inconsistency is currently most obvious in the federal
system, where the U.S. Court of Appeals for the Ninth Circuit
has twenty-eight judges and three other circuits have fifteen or
more judges each.

Large intermediate courts, both state and federal—whether
regional or statewide—seek to maintain intra-court consistency
with the rule that a decision of any panel binds all other panels

until it is overturned by the supreme court, or by an en banc decision of the intermediate court itself (if that court has such a procedure). The theory is that each panel speaks in the name of the court; its opinion is the court's opinion. While this rule fosters stability and predictability in the law, it also leads to some rather refined and strained distinctions by panels seeking to avoid the force of a prior holding.

The federal appellate courts can employ the en banc device to iron out their internal conflicts, but such a procedure is not provided for in some state appellate courts. In the federal courts an en banc hearing can occur at one of two points. One is before any panel has decided the appeal. That might occur when the appeal is perceived as presenting an unusually important question that the court as a whole should address. The other point is after a panel decision. An en banc rehearing might then be perceived as desirable if the panel decision conflicts with a prior decision of another panel, or puts the court in conflict with another court of appeals, or presents an especially important issue that the whole court should settle. At either point any of the court's judges can suggest an en banc, but the proceeding will be pursued only if a majority of the judges vote for it. After a panel decision a party can suggest a rehearing en banc.

Although the en banc can be an effective device for maintaining internal harmony on a large intermediate court, federal appellate judges tend to disfavor it. On these busy courts the judges are fully occupied with hearing and deciding appeals in their three-judge panels; having to sit en banc interferes with their normal work and draws off time and energy from their regular duties. If the en banc is a rehearing after a panel decision, it amounts to another appellate level in the judicial system—a duplicating review. Moreover, in the larger courts the proceeding is awkward. When a dozen or more judges must sit on the bench together, the asking of questions during oral argument is difficult. Decisional conferences take longer in order to give every judge an opportunity to speak, and there is an increased likelihood of numerous concurring and dissenting opinions.

To ameliorate some of these difficulties, Congress has enacted a statute authorizing any court of appeals with more than fifteen judges to sit en banc with fewer than all of them, in such number as the court may fix by rule. The Ninth Circuit is the only court thus far using this "limited en banc." That court's rule sets the en banc court at eleven judges—the chief judge plus ten drawn at random. Because this is less than a majority, provision is made for a majority to require a rehearing before the entire court; however, this provision has never been invoked.

In large judicial systems the subject-matter style of court organization—which has thus far gained only limited acceptance in the United States—has a potential for maintaining doctrinal coherence in the intermediate level beyond that which can be attained under regional organization or through rotating panels with random docket assignments. A high degree of uniformity can be achieved through this type of organization because appeals routed to a subject-matter court are not decided by any other intermediate court; the jurisdiction in the subject-matter forum is exclusive, so there can be no conflict with a co-equal court.

The subject-matter concept can also be employed within a large intermediate court to avoid the possibility of intra-court conflict. Panels can be organized on a subject-matter basis, with the docket divided among them. Probably the only example of this in an American appellate court is the so-called "oil and gas

panel" in the U.S. Fifth Circuit. It came about because most of
the court's judges had to recuse themselves (refrain from
participation) in oil and gas cases because of their ownership of
interests in those enterprises. Thus all such appeals were routed
to the small group of judges with no potential conflict of interest.
Apparently this panel has functioned satisfactorily over a long
period of years.

E.   Relationships Between State and Federal Appellate Courts

Under the distinctively American variety of federalism,
complete top-to-bottom judicial systems exist in both state and
federal realms. The fifty state judicial pyramids (plus those of the
District of Columbia and Puerto Rico) with their trial and
appellate courts function alongside the federal pyramid which also
contains both trial and appellate forums. Most litigation
commenced in a state judicial system is concluded there without
any involvement by federal courts. The reverse is true to an even
higher degree; nearly all litigation initiated in the federal courts
terminates without any state court involvement. Yet there are
some state-federal linkages and points of impingement.

At the appellate level, there is one direct link between the
state and federal systems. By Act of Congress, pursuant to Art.
III of the Constitution, the U.S. Supreme Court has jurisdiction
to review decisions on federal law made by "the highest court of
a State in which a decision could be had." The "highest court"
for this purpose is normally the state supreme court, but it could
be a state intermediate court or even a trial court. It is the
highest court to which, under state law, the particular case could
be carried.

As the result of a judicial gloss put on this statute, the Supreme Court's jurisdiction is limited to those state decisions in which federal law is not merely decided but is controlling. This limitation has given rise to the doctrine of the "adequate and independent state ground." If the state judgment rests on a state law ground adequate to support it wholly apart from the federal ground, there is no authority in the Supreme Court to review it. Put another way, a federal question is controlling for this purpose if a reversal of the state court's decision on the federal question would result in a reversal of the judgment. If the judgment would remain in force after a reversal on the federal ground, the Supreme Court lacks jurisdiction. To decide the federal question in that circumstance would be a meaningless act, as the decision would have no effect on the rights of the litigants.

The proportion of state supreme court decisions subject to U.S. Supreme Court review has increased substantially. One study showed that from 1959 to 1979 the number of federal questions involved in state supreme court cases grew threefold. Another survey indicated that in 1983 more than a quarter of all state supreme court decisions involved federal law.

Two developments explain this growth. One is the pattern of Supreme Court interpretations of the Fourteenth Amendment, beginning in the 1960s, expanding the range of federal constitutional rights available to state criminal defendants. As a result, much of the state criminal process has been federalized, requiring state courts to decide a wide array of federal questions in that field. The other explanation is that Congress has been active over the years in creating new federal causes of action for damages and other relief that can be asserted in state as well as federal courts. Thus, on both the civil and criminal sides of the docket, state supreme courts decide many more federal questions than they did several decades ago, thereby opening up more of their decisions to U.S. Supreme Court review.

In relation to the U.S. Supreme Court, on matters of federal law the state supreme courts are, in effect, in the position of intermediate appellate courts; they do not have the last say on federal matters, although in practice the Supreme Court can review only a small percentage of their decisions. (With respect to matters of state law, state supreme courts are, of course, courts of last resort.) Certiorari petitions seeking review of federal questions in state cases account for about a quarter of the Supreme Court's docket annually.

Although the Supreme Court's exercise of the above-described jurisdiction is the only federal appellate review available for state decisions, state criminal cases can be indirectly reviewed in federal courts under certain circumstances through the writ of habeas corpus. However, that is not an appellate review in the usual sense; it is classified as "collateral review." It is a new, independent civil action initiated in a U.S. district court attacking the legality of detention. The proceeding is not necessarily limited to a scrutiny of the state record, as would be the case with appellate review; the federal district court can hold a "de novo evidentiary hearing," receiving fresh evidence and trying the federal issues as though no previous hearing had occurred. A district court decision in a habeas corpus case can be appealed to a U.S. court of appeals and is ultimately reviewable by the Supreme Court. Many regard this collateral system of review as redundant and wasteful of judicial resources; others consider it a necessary avenue for protecting the constitutional rights of persons in state custody.

While the U.S Supreme Court is empowered to correct

errors of federal law made by state courts, there is no corresponding authority in state courts to correct errors of state law made by federal courts. State courts have no jurisdiction to review federal judgments. The state-federal judicial relationship is thus asymmetrical. However, so-called certification procedures provide a means whereby issues of state law in cases pending in federal courts can be put before the state court of last resort for authoritative resolution. The availability of such a procedure depends entirely on state law. Thirty-nine states have statutes or rules of court authorizing federal courts, in their discretion, to certify to the state supreme court issues of state law. In some states the certification can be made by any federal court; in others, only a federal appellate court can certify. The certification sends a specific state law question to the state court, with such information or as much of the record as is needed for its decision. The federal court holds the case on its docket pending receipt of an answer, after which the federal litigation proceeds in light of the state court's ruling. This procedure can cause delay and expense, but it does obviate a federal court's making an unreviewable state law determination that may turn out to be incorrect as revealed by later state court decisions.

CHAPTER THREE

ACCESS TO APPELLATE COURTS: WHEN, FOR WHOM, HOW MUCH

Access to the decision-making authority of appellate courts is governed by a mixture of statutes, rules of court, and case law. This body of law serves the important function of defining the limits of appellate power and the relationship of an appellate court to the trial courts under its jurisdiction. The access doctrines, as they are referred to collectively, are of great concern to lawyers seeking to take a case from the trial to the appellate level. The doctrines are also of central concern to appellate judges, who must apply them so as to exercise only the authority they are given under the legal order.

There are three aspects to the subject of appellate court access, expressed in shorthand as problems of when, for whom, and how much. Each is discussed below.

These problems concern access to the first level of review—whether that be in an intermediate appellate court or in a court of last resort—where review is accorded as a matter of right. That right, however, is qualified by the access doctrines. Sometimes in three-tiered judicial systems contested issues over access in the intermediate court get carried forward like other legal issues to the upper level for authoritative resolution.

A.   When—Appealability

The question of "when" concerns the point in the trial court proceedings at which the case may be taken up to the appellate court for review. A case initiated in a trial court progresses through several stages, typically extending over weeks or months. In a civil action there is first the exchange of pleadings between the adversaries, then discovery is often pursued, along with the filing of motions of various kinds, pretrial conferences, and finally the trial and decision. In criminal cases there is the arraignment, followed by grand jury proceedings, assorted motions, and eventually the trial and decision. The last step in the trial court is the entry of judgment concluding the entire matter at that level. Along the way in both civil and criminal cases there are usually numerous rulings by the trial judge, many of which are objected to by one side or the other. At what point may a party complaining about any of those rulings obtain appellate review? May a ruling be appealed immediately after it is made, or must the complaining party wait until the whole case is terminated? This problem is labeled as one of appealability. It is a matter of the timing of review, not whether the ruling may be reviewed at all. The latter is a problem of reviewability, discussed below in Section C, Part 1.

1.   The Finality Doctrine and Its Permutations

A final judgment concluding the entire case, with nothing more to be done by the trial court, is always appealable. The insistence on a final decision as a prerequisite for appeal rests on several considerations of efficient and fair judicial administration.

The finality doctrine embodies a policy against piecemeal review. Time and resources of the appellate court and the litigants are usually saved by postponing review until the conclusion of the trial court proceeding and then placing the entire case before the appellate court at once. Allowing appeals at earlier points would often result in more than one appeal in the same case. Multiple appeals require the parties to prepare multiple sets of briefs and pursue more than once the procedural steps to put the matter properly before the appellate court; they also require the court to revisit the case repeatedly.

Moreover, a party complaining about a ruling at the time it is made may ultimately win the case and thus have nothing to complain about. In addition, a ruling that seems problematic immediately after it is made may turn out to be harmless when viewed in the context of the whole proceeding. Thus the final decision rule works to prevent unnecessary appeals.

The rule also functions to keep appellate courts out of trial court business, leaving trial judges free to conduct proceedings without the interruptions that would be caused by appeals along the way.

Questions can arise as to when a particular adjudication is "final" and thus appealable under final decision statutes. A general rule is that the judgment must end the litigation on its merits. An order denying certification of a plaintiff class in an attempted class action, for example, does not meet the test because members of the putative class can continue the action as individuals. It is said that there is no appealable judgment if any significant matter remains for determination by the trial court. A judgment may be considered final, however, if all that remains are so-called ministerial actions. For example, a decree canceling conveyances and ordering property returned to the plaintiff is appealable even though an accounting must still be accomplished.

Also, a decision on the merits is final although a claim for attorney's fees remains for adjudication. Finality is viewed in a practical rather than a conceptualistic light. The Supreme Court, for instance, held final a district court order staying a case on its docket pending resolution of a state court action involving the same controversy, on the reasoning that the stay order effectively ended the federal litigation because the state case would settle the matter, leaving nothing to litigate in the federal court.

Pressures are put on the final decision rule by litigants seeking access to the appellate court before the trial proceeding has run its course. In certain instances fairness and common sense do seem to call for immediate review. Responding to those considerations, courts sometimes give strained interpretations to the concept of finality. Such decisions have often produced ambiguity in the doctrine, illustrating the proposition that hard cases make bad law. A party, unsure after studying the case law about the meaning of "final," may feel compelled to appeal at a certain point for fear that if no appeal is then taken the court will later hold that there had been a final decision at that point and by then the time for appeal will have expired, thus foreclosing all opportunity to obtain review. Such premature appeals are taken out of an abundance of caution stemming from decisions that, in an attempt to reach a just result, generate uncertainty about what is "final."

A more rational response in the federal appellate courts has been the development of the "collateral order" doctrine as a judicial gloss on the final decision rule. To be appealable under this doctrine as a "final" decision, without waiting for conclusion of the entire case, an order must involve a matter clearly separable from the merits of the case, must conclusively settle the matter, and must be such that an eventual appeal from a judgment terminating the entire case would be ineffective to protect the party's rights. Orders that have been held appealable under that doctrine include orders denying the defendant's motion to require the plaintiff to post security for costs as a prerequisite to a stockholder's derivative action, denying a petition to proceed in forma pauperis, imposing on defendants ninety percent of the costs of notifying members of a plaintiff class, and rejecting a state agency's claim of Eleventh Amendment immunity from suit. In effect, such orders are treated as a separate unit of litigation for purposes of applying the finality requirement.

In response to practical pressures on the finality doctrine, the unit of litigation has been further redefined through a judicially promulgated rule. Rule 54 of the Federal Rules of Civil Procedure, copied by many states, addresses the situation that may occur when there is more than one claim in the action or more than one party on either side of the case. If the trial court makes a final decision as to one or more but fewer than all the claims or as to one or more but fewer than all the parties and also determines that there is no just cause for delay in permitting an appeal, the decision is appealable. This rule is a recognition that much modern litigation is multi-claim and multi-party and that under the liberal rules of claim and party joinder some parts of the case are quite unrelated to others; thus, they can be treated as separate cases for appeal purposes.

In the federal courts, the concept of finality could undergo a substantial reworking as the result of a statute enacted by Congress in 1990. This amendment to the Rules Enabling Act authorizes the Supreme Court to define when a ruling is final. Thus the extensive case law on this subject could be clarified by written rule, with the possibility of redefinition from time to time in light of experience and the needs of justice.

2. Interlocutory Appeals and Extraordinary Writs

Although there are solid justifications for generally requiring finality in trial court proceedings as a prerequisite for access to an appellate court, there are nevertheless circumstances in which permitting an immediate appeal from certain trial rulings that do not end the case—referred to as interlocutory orders—may serve the interests of fairness and efficiency. American judicial systems vary in the degree to which they allow appeals from such orders.

Theoretically, two extreme positions could be taken, at opposite ends of a spectrum. At one end, a rule could preclude an appeal until entry of a truly final judgment concluding all aspects of the case. At the other end, a rule could allow an appeal immediately after any ruling of the trial judge. No American jurisdiction takes either of these positions; they are all somewhere along the spectrum in between.

The federal system is perhaps as close as any to the finality end of the spectrum. From the beginning the federal courts have stressed the policy, embodied in the United States Code, favoring finality of decision as a precondition for appellate review. Section 1292(a) of Title 28 specifies only a small number of interlocutory orders that are immediately appealable. These include orders granting, modifying, or refusing injunctions; orders appointing receivers or refusing to terminate receiverships; and orders determining the rights and liabilities of parties in admiralty cases.

New York probably comes closer than any other jurisdiction to the opposite end of the appealability spectrum. Its statutes permit appeals from a wide range of interim trial rulings, including determinations that a state statute is unconstitutional and orders concerning a provisional remedy, involving some part of the merits, or affecting a substantial right. Statutes in most other states permit fewer interlocutory appeals than this but more than are permitted under the federal statute.

In deciding as a matter of policy the extent to which appellate review should be allowed for non-final trial court rulings, a legislature must balance competing considerations. On the one hand, all the justifications underlying the finality doctrine weigh against interlocutory appeals. On the other hand, practical considerations of judicial administration often make it sensible to permit review before finality is reached.

Consider, as one example of the problem, an order denying a defendant's motion to dismiss the complaint for failure to state a claim upon which relief can be granted. If the motion is well taken, and the trial judge has incorrectly denied it, immediate appellate review could obviate the need for any further proceedings, a potential savings of weeks or months of pretrial and trial litigation with all of the attendant expense. An appeal, however, would be costly and time-consuming and may be fruitless, particularly with today's procedural rules allowing liberal amendment of complaints. Whether to allow such an appeal is a debatable judgment call; most systems do not allow one.

The extent to which interlocutory appeals are permitted is based in part on the degree to which the system trusts its trial judges. A high degree of respect for the competence and fairness of those judges makes interlocutory appeals seem relatively unnecessary. A low level of regard inspires the view that parties should have greater access to the appellate court to permit that court to monitor and correct trial judges at interim stages. Thus the rules governing interlocutory appeals can be a gauge of the legislators' view of their trial judges.

In addition to specifying certain types of interlocutory rulings that are immediately appealable, statutes also typically provide for discretionary review of unspecified rulings. An example in the federal system is 28 U.S.C. § 1292(b), which provides that in making an otherwise unappealable interlocutory ruling the trial judge may certify that the ruling involves a controlling question of law, the prompt resolution of which may materially advance the termination of the action; the appellate court may then in its discretion review the order. The wording of this statute defines the circumstances under which discretionary review may be accorded. In some states the court's discretion is not so qualified; the statute simply provides that any interim ruling may be reviewed in the discretion of either the trial judge or the appellate court, or sometimes only if both concur. Details vary from one state to another. All of these discretionary statutes, whatever their wording, rest on the premise that there will be unforeseen circumstances in which prompt review of an interim ruling is desirable, and that the courts should be empowered to deal with them on a case-by-case basis. How the courts exercise this discretionary control over access to the appellate level will be influenced by their attitude toward the considerations underlying the finality doctrine as well as by the equities of the situation.

Beyond these various statutory authorizations for interlocutory appeals, there is the possibility of obtaining review through an extraordinary writ. Writs such as mandamus and prohibition were developed in the English common law as means by which a court could control an inferior tribunal by commanding action that the law required and forbidding action that the law did not authorize. Those writs were inherited in America along with the rest of the common law. They are available today in many states and in the federal system. The extent to which appellate courts use them to allow interlocutory review varies considerably from one jurisdiction to another, and even within a single jurisdiction usage is not always consistent or principled.

In the U.S. courts of appeals, litigants have been able to obtain review by mandamus of orders striking a demand for jury trial, transferring a case to a district outside the circuit, and appointing a special master. The statutory authorization for such usage is 28 U.S.C. § 1651, the so-called All Writs Act, providing that federal appellate courts "may issue all writs necessary or appropriate in aid of" their jurisdiction. Sometimes when those courts permit interlocutory review by mandamus it is not easy to see how such review is "necessary or appropriate" in aid of appellate jurisdiction, the only jurisdiction they possess.

California has an unusually liberal practice of permitting review by an extraordinary writ whenever the appellate court believes the matter to be of sufficient importance to justify immediate appellate scrutiny. The more an appellate court moves in that direction, the more it undercuts the legislative scheme governing interlocutory appeals.

In some states, for example Arizona, the legislature has abolished the common-law writs and put in their place a statutory proceeding denominated a "special action." The considerations involved in administering such a procedure are similar to those involved in administering the common-law writs.

To sum up the foregoing rules, if the adjudication meets the requirements of the final decision rule (as elaborated upon by the collateral order doctrine and, in most judicial systems, by a Rule 54-type provision), it is appealable; if it does not, but it is a type of interlocutory order specified by statute as appealable, it is appealable. If the order is not appealable under any of those provisions, the litigant may ask the court to permit a discretionary appeal or, as a last resort, seek review through an extraordinary writ, provided that such procedures are available in the jurisdiction. All of the above rules operate together to govern the point at which a litigant can obtain access to the appellate court. To put it another way, they determine when the appellate court can interfere with a trial court proceeding.

B. For Whom—Standing to Appeal

Not everyone is in position to obtain appellate review of a case. Appellate courts, like courts generally in the Anglo-American legal world, sit to resolve real controversies between adverse parties. In order to gain access to an appellate court, one must exhibit a continuing, live dispute in which something is at stake for the would-be appellant. This requirement is sometimes spoken of as a requirement that the appellant have "standing to appeal." Like the "when" doctrines just discussed, this is a gatekeeping doctrine, regulating access to appellate review. The concept is analogous to that of standing to litigate at the trial level.

The general rule is that any "aggrieved party" may appeal. That is, one who is a party to the trial court proceeding and who is adversely affected by the trial court's action may invoke the appellate court's reviewing power.

The typical appellant is the litigant against whom judgment has been entered. However, parties in other circumstances have been allowed to appeal. For example, a plaintiff who prevailed on the merits but received less than the relief sought has been held to be an "aggrieved party." A defendant has been permitted to appeal a summary judgment in favor of a co-defendant against whom he had claimed a right of contribution. On the other hand, the Supreme Court held that a member of a school board, even though named in the complaint as a defendant, could not appeal from a judgment against the board because the judgment was only against the board as an entity and not against any of its members individually.

Normally an appeal may be taken only by one who was actually joined as a party or who intervened in the trial court. In some circumstances, however, a non-party may be accorded standing to appeal. The general test is, as with parties, whether the would-be appellant is "aggrieved" by the trial court's ruling. For example, non-party news gathering organizations were allowed to appeal an order closing a criminal trial to the news media. However, an attorney was not permitted to appeal a judgment adverse to his client even though the attorney's fee was dependent upon the client's obtaining recovery.

C. *How Much—Breadth and Depth of Review*

Assuming that the case is properly in the appellate court, *i.e.*, that the appellate court has authority to review the case under the "when" rules, and that the appellant has standing under the "for whom" rules, attention is then focused on identifying the issues in the case that are open for review and the degree of scrutiny to be given those issues by the appellate court.

The first involves the breadth of review—or scope of review; the second involves the depth of review—or standards of review. These will be discussed in that order.

1.   Scope of Review

As noted in Chapter 1, an important characteristic of American appellate practice is the controlling force accorded to the record, the documents and formal written transcript from the trial proceedings. The general proposition, subject to qualifications discussed below, is that an appellate court considers only those facts that were established at trial and reviews only those questions that were properly raised and preserved in the trial court, as evidenced by the record. This deeply entrenched notion in American appellate courts led Professor Roscoe Pound to accuse them in the early 1900s of "record worship."

As a result, advocates in courts of first instance must be attentive to accomplishing two objectives simultaneously: they must attempt to persuade the court to decide the case in favor of their clients, and they must, at the same time, make sure that the written record shows the facts essential to their case as well as all of their objections to the various rulings of the trial judge, in order for all possible contentions to be available for review in the event of an appeal.

There are two possible exceptions to the controlling force of the record insofar as facts are concerned. One is that the appellate court, like a trial court, may take judicial notice of certain facts that are of common knowledge in the jurisdiction and are not reasonably subject to dispute. The other exception is that the appellate court has discretion to consider, in the interest of justice, a fact not in the record that is conveyed by counsel during oral argument and not disputed by opposing counsel.

An important reason for an appellate court's general refusal to consider issues not raised below is the incompleteness of the record on such issues. In the nature of things, neither party is likely to have introduced evidence relevant to issues not raised at trial. Thus the appellate court has no factual basis, or at best a shaky basis, on which to make a decision. Also, the appellate court lacks the benefit of the trial judge's views on the matter, views that might contribute to a sounder appellate resolution.

The practice of not considering issues for the first time at the appellate level also encourages finality in litigation. Appellate insistence on that rule forces counsel to take care to raise all possible issues during the trial when they can be heard and decided—perhaps to all parties' satisfaction so that no one will appeal. Without the rule, litigants might, either deliberately or unwittingly, omit an issue in the trial court; if they lost at trial, they would have a second chance on a new issue at the appellate level. Not only would finality be eroded by such a practice, but there would also be an unfairness in making the trial winner undergo a second round of litigation on a matter that could have been litigated in the first round.

Appellate courts sometimes relax the general rule of refusing to consider issues not raised below. For example, an appellate court may decide an issue initially presented to it that is purely one of law. The lack of an evidentiary record is not a problem; the facts of the case are the same as they would be if the legal issue had been raised in the trial court. Although the appellate court still is deprived of the trial judge's views, the need for efficient administration of justice may outweigh that concern. Relevant considerations include how meritorious the appellant's argument is and the importance of settling the issue in light of foreseeable future litigation.

Appellate courts may also relax the general rule in situations of "plain error." In these cases, the trial court's mistake is clear from the record, which is sufficiently developed to permit an informed appellate decision, and failure to reverse would, in the appellate court's judgment, work a substantial injustice. A plain error may be noticed and acted upon by the court sua sponte (on its own motion) even if no party has raised it in the trial or appellate court.

Normally a party who has tried a case on one legal theory and lost is not permitted to shift to a new theory in the appellate court in order to achieve a different result. However, in some instances a plaintiff who has prevailed in the trial court on a theory that the appellate court thereafter finds to be legally insufficient has been permitted to assert another theory on appeal and thereby obtain a reversal with an opportunity to reestablish a right of recovery on the new theory. In order to give the plaintiff this kind of second bite at the apple, the appellate court must be able to discern from the record a possible basis of recovery; if it does, then the interest in affording a remedy when the law and facts warrant it overrides the interests served by the rule against entertaining new issues and theories on appeal. The court is, in effect, saving the plaintiff from poor lawyering. In rare instances, the court might affirm on the new theory instead of remanding for a new trial. Such a disposition is rare because of the substantial potential for unfairness to the defendant, who was not on notice during the trial that the plaintiff would rely on the new theory and thus would not have developed a defense.

At the opposite end of the spectrum from "plain error" is the concept of "harmless error." Here, although an erroneous trial ruling appears in the record, the appellate court deems the error not prejudicial to the substantial rights of the appellant. The tests for identifying harmless errors are not always clear or consistent. The concept rests on the awareness that a trial judge's ruling, though legally erroneous, does not always have an adverse impact on a litigant's interests. Another way of putting this is to say that the error made no difference; viewed in the totality of the trial court proceedings, it did not affect the outcome. Many errors along the way in a trial proceeding are of this sort, and it makes no sense to reverse the judgment because of them.

The controlling force accorded to the record and the resistance to considering new questions and theories on appeal by American appellate courts find their origin in the writ of error in the English common-law courts. At common law there was no concept of an appeal like that in the modern-day United States. Instead, a party against whom a judgment had been rendered at nisi prius could seek a writ of error from the court at West-minster, assigning specified errors of law committed by the trial judge. The proceeding, in effect, made the trial judge a defendant. Under that procedure the judge could not have been guilty of error unless a matter had been presented to him and he had ruled on it.

In light of that history it is curious that the term "appeal," now in universal usage in this country, came out of equity, which had quite a different concept of review. In equity practice there was no concern about assigning errors on the part of the first-instance judge. Rather, the review was of the whole case in an effort to reach the right decision, to do equity.

Although alien to most American appellate institutions, that practice is familiar in other countries. An approach to review of that sort can be seen in the German appellate courts known as *Oberlandesgerichte* and in the English Court of Appeal, Criminal Division. Such de novo review of the case is not completely unheard of in the United States. California statutes, for example, authorize the appellate court to receive new evidence and to make factual determinations different from those made by the trial court. That authority, however, is exercised sparingly. If exercised more freely, it would transform the appellate court from an agency for review of what happened in the lower court into a forum for the re-trial of cases. Although there may be some attraction to that role by appellate courts striving to serve the interests of justice in each case, it would raise serious questions as to the most appropriate allocation of judicial functions and resources.

2.   *Standards of Review*

When an issue is properly before an appellate court for decision, the court must make a threshold determination of what standard of review to apply. This is a problem of the appropriate depth of review, of how deep-cutting the appellate scrutiny will be, of how much deference, if any, will be given to the trial court's decision. The possibilities range from none to almost total deference. For this purpose, trial court rulings have been conventionally categorized into three types: law, fact, and discretion. In addition there is the so-called mixed law-fact determination. Each of these is discussed below.

Questions of Law. For purely legal questions, no deference at all is accorded to the trial court's ruling. The customary proposition is that an appellate court will decide questions of law de novo, reviewing the matter independently and reaching its own decision as though the trial court decision did not exist. The trial court's advantage of having heard firsthand the testimony of witnesses as to the facts has no bearing on the determination of a question of law.

The justification for this de novo authority derives from one of the major reasons for the existence of appellate courts: to maintain uniformity in the law throughout the jurisdiction and to keep the law evolving and developing in the common-law style. This appellate role would be impaired if the courts lacked authority to enunciate legal rules independently.

Questions of Fact. These must be divided into two types for purposes of appellate review: factual determinations made by a judge in a non-jury trial, and factual issues resolved by a jury.

The standard of review most commonly applied to a trial judge's factual findings is that prescribed by Rule 52(a) of the Federal Rules of Civil Procedure, widely copied by the states. The rule provides in pertinent part that a judge's "[f]indings of fact, whether based on oral or documentary evidence, shall not be set aside unless clearly erroneous, and due regard shall be given to the opportunity of the trial court to judge of the credibility of the witnesses." This is referred to as the "clearly erroneous" standard. It calls for a considerable measure of deference by the appellate court to the trial judge's decision on any question of fact. In other words, unlike its role in relation to a legal question, the appellate court is not free to reach its own independent decision on a factual issue.

The rule prescribing the clearly erroneous standard is important in allocating functions between the trial and appellate levels in the judicial system. It assigns to trial courts the primary fact-determining role, placing appellate courts in a back-up role that leaves them more energy and resources to devote to the resolution of legal questions, which is their primary mission. This standard of review is based in large part on the reality that trial judges are in a better position than appellate judges to resolve factual disputes; they are present throughout the reception of the evidence and have the opportunity, which appellate judges do not have, to evaluate the credibility of witnesses whom they can see and hear, a circumstance emphasized expressly in the rule. The importance of keeping appellate judges out of the fact-finding business is underscored by the rule's provision that even if the evidence is entirely documentary, with the demeanor factor therefore absent, the clearly erroneous standard still applies.

The differing standards of review applied to legal and factual questions make it critical to determine into which category a particular issue falls. Of all the unclear lines in our jurisprudence, the law-fact line can be among the unclearest. There are, of course, some situations in which the line is sharp. Questions as to who did what, where, and when, *i.e.*, what happened, are described as basic or historical facts and are unambiguously treated as questions of fact. Questions as to the content of a legal rule, *i.e.*, the pertinent legal doctrine to be applied, are easily seen as questions of law.

An inference of ultimate fact drawn from basic facts is usually treated as a factual determination. An example is whether, given the circumstances surrounding a person's behavior, one can infer that the person was intoxicated.

Murkier terrain is encountered when the inference from basic facts involves a legal standard. This kind of problem shades into the problem of the so-called mixed law-fact questions discussed in the next section. In a 1982 case, the U.S. Supreme Court held that whether a company's seniority plan was devised with "an intention to discriminate" on racial grounds, something expressly prohibited by a statute, was a factual question, even though it was an ultimate fact and its determination controlled the company's liability under the statute. The Court said that Rule 52(a) made no distinction between basic facts and ultimate facts, and that deference must be given to the trial judge's findings on both.

An appellate court's task of sorting out law from fact for review purposes is similar to the task confronting a trial judge in a jury trial, who must make this classification so that factual issues may be submitted to the jury while questions of law are reserved for the judge. In a non-jury case, issues decided by the judge that would have been submitted to the jury had there been one are generally considered factual issues by an appellate court for purposes of applying the clearly erroneous standard.

The law-fact distinction in most cases has long been settled by custom or precedent. When it has not, there is no rule that can clearly distinguish law from fact. To a considerable extent the distinction is based on the practical consideration of which decision maker is in the superior position to decide the question, bearing in mind the primary functions assigned to each. If a decision involves an assessment of the credibility of witnesses, including observation of their demeanor, and draws upon practical experiences in life, it is likely to be classified as one of fact.

Assuming that the question is identified as one of fact, how is the appellate court to decide whether the trial judge's finding is "clearly erroneous"? The test is not whether in the appellate court's view the trial judge was incorrect or whether the appellate judges would have decided the matter differently if they had been sitting at trial. An often-stated formula is this: Even though there is evidence to support the finding, a trial judge's factual determination will be deemed clearly erroneous if the appellate court, after considering the entire record, is left with the definite and firm conviction that a mistake has been made. This standard obviously leaves considerable room for judgment on the part of appellate judges, but it does indicate that mere disagreement with the trial judge's view of the facts is not sufficient. Rather, because fact finding is primarily a trial court function, the judge's findings come to the appellate court with a high degree of immunity from reversal, and a heavy burden rests on an advocate who seeks to overturn them.

Aside from the above formulation, a finding will be deemed clearly erroneous if there is no evidence or insufficient evidence in the record to support it, as a matter of law. Also, the finding will be overturned on appeal if the trial judge made it under a misapprehension as to the correct law.

A jury's findings of fact are reviewed under a far more lenient standard, reflecting the extraordinary deference paid to juries in the American legal order. The Seventh Amendment to the U.S. Constitution, governing jury trials in federal courts, provides that no fact found by a jury "shall be otherwise re-examined in any Court of the United States, than according to the rules of the common law." Similar notions obtain in the state courts. Under the "rules of the common law," judicial examination of jury verdicts is generally limited to determining whether the evidence in the record is sufficient to support the finding, *i.e.*, whether there is evidence from which reasonable minds could have reached the conclusion reached by the jury.

Thus an appellate court may overturn a judge's finding even though there is evidence to support it, but it may not do so with a jury verdict. In other words, a fact found by a judge could be set aside when the same fact found by a jury on the same evidence would be upheld. It is paradoxical that the standards of review give much more deference to the jury than to the judge. A judge is typically a law-trained person with substantial experience in evaluating conflicting testimony and arriving at factual conclusions from a tangled web of data. The jury, by contrast, is composed of legally untrained persons drawn at random from the community, with no experience at fact finding. Given these relative competencies, one would think that the practice would be the opposite of what it is, that more deference would be accorded to the trial judge than to the jury. The explanation seems to lie in the special importance attached to the role of the jury in American life and law.

Mixed Questions of Law and Fact. Under Rule 52(a) all questions are classified as either of law or of fact. There is, by the terms of the rule, no third possibility, no hybrid "mixed" questions. Yet appellate courts frequently speak of these and struggle to decide whether to review them de novo, as legal issues, or under the clearly erroneous standard, as factual issues. This problem arises when the trial decision under review involves the application of a legal rule to a set of facts.

Litigation involves many questions in which factual and legal elements are thus intertwined, *e.g.,* whether the defendant's conduct (factual matters) amounts to negligence (a legal standard), or whether the activities of several manufacturers constitute a conspiracy in restraint of trade. Most such questions are reviewed de novo as matters of law. However, negligence has long been viewed as an issue of fact; in a jury trial it would be submitted to the jury. As noted above, if precedent has not already defined the category, there is no clear test to be applied.

A so-called functional approach has been developed for the analysis of mixed questions. If a question is heavily dependent on factual ingredients that a trial judge is in a superior position to assess because the determination draws on the "mainsprings of human conduct," it is treated as a question of fact. On the other hand, if its resolution implicates values and policies of general concern and involves a matter as to which there should be jurisdiction-wide uniformity, it is treated as a question of law. In a much-cited 1984 opinion the U.S. Court of Appeals for the Ninth Circuit took this functional approach, deciding that whether "exigent circumstances" existed, excusing law enforcement agents from the knock-before-entering requirement relating to searches, presented a question of law and hence would be given de novo review.

Constitutional questions are often of the mixed variety: Do the facts as to the interrogation of a criminal defendant—length, availability of breaks, food, sleep, etc.—make a resulting confession "involuntary" and hence in violation of the Due Process Clause? In a suit for defamation, does the evidence show "actual malice" so as to overcome a First Amendment defense? These and like questions are sometimes referred to as questions of "constitutional fact," but they are nevertheless dealt with as legal questions. The explanation is that the "ultimate fact" or conclusion to be drawn from the basic facts is what determines whether there has been a constitutional violation and that the interest in uniform, effective enforcement of the Constitution requires de novo appellate review.

Discretionary Rulings by the Trial Court. On matters

entrusted to its discretion, a trial court has considerable freedom to go either way without being reversed; appellate deference is at its maximum. Indeed, the very term "discretion" means that there is choice, that there is no "correct" or "incorrect" decision as far as the appellate court is concerned. Trial court discretion, however, is not absolute; the appellate court remains in ultimate control. The standard under which a discretionary ruling is reviewed on appeal is "abuse of discretion" or "arbitrariness," a much more deferential standard of review than "clearly erroneous." A trial judge, in other words, has a large field within which to go in different directions, but there are boundaries; the appellate court's role is to patrol the outer limits.

By what test does an appellate court determine whether an abuse of discretion has occurred? Formulations of the standard vary. It has been said that an appellate court should find an abuse of discretion only if it is firmly convinced, upon a weighing of the relevant factors, that the trial judge committed a clear error of judgment. Abuse may also be found if the reviewing court believes that the ruling has worked a gross injustice or is outrageous or unconscionable. Some courts have said that they will not find abuse if reasonable persons could differ as to the propriety of the trial judge's actions. At times appellate courts have upheld trial court discretionary actions while figuratively holding their noses, making it plain that they disagree and would not have acted the same way.

Curiously and confusingly, all discretion is not alike. In the multitude of matters committed to trial court discretion, the degree of choice left to the trial judge varies depending upon the stringency with which the appellate court applies the "abuse" standard. Professor Maurice Rosenberg has suggested that the leeway allowed a trial judge can be expressed in terms of grades of discretion, from Grade A to Grade D.

Grade A gives maximum freedom of choice to the trial judge; an appellate court will rarely, if ever, find abuse. Included in this category is a wide array of actions in managing litigation: rulings on discovery motions, setting and conducting pretrial conferences, granting or refusing continuances, controlling the length and nature of examination and cross-examination of witnesses, deciding whether to require a general or a special verdict, and so on. The legal system has placed the trial judge in charge of the trial court proceedings, and appellate courts will not undertake micro-management of the process. They are not in a good position to do so, and they have better uses for their time. Also, these are matters on which it would be difficult, if not impossible, to formulate any meaningful rules by which to measure the correctness of a trial judge's actions.

Grades B and C allow somewhat less running room for the trial court. Orders denying leave to amend pleadings and rulings on forum non conveniens motions fall into these lower levels.

Grade D discretion is not much discretion at all. For example, in reviewing a decision to withhold or grant a declaratory judgment, supposedly a matter of trial court discretion, appellate courts give little deference, treating the matter almost as if it were a question of law subject to de novo review.

A particular matter may start out within the Grade A category but over time sink to a lower grade. Judge Henry Friendly cited as an example of this phenomenon the evolution in appellate review of trial rulings on whether a party in a civil action would be permitted to make a late demand for jury trial, a matter said to be within the trial court's discretion. As time passed and judges ruled on many late jury demands a pattern emerged, a framework within which such rulings could be evaluated. The trial judges' range of choices was accordingly narrowed by practice; deviations from the established pattern could be seen as an abuse of discretion, and appellate control over this matter was thus increased.

Standards of review are applied by an appellate court on an issue-by-issue basis, not to the case as a whole. An appeal presenting more than one issue for review might involve more than one standard. Some issues might be governed by the de novo standard, some by the clearly erroneous standard, and others by the abuse of discretion standard. Before addressing any issue the court needs to know the applicable standard of review; otherwise, it has no guidance as to how to approach the issue.

Appellate courts seem to have become increasingly sensitive in recent years to the importance of a clear under-standing as to the appropriate standard. Indeed, many courts now require counsel expressly to identify the applicable standard at the outset of the argument of each issue presented for review. That requirement has the salutary effect of forcing the advocates to shape the argument in light of the standard of review to be applied. Each of the standards calls for a distinctive kind of argument. Appellate counsel hoping to prevail on a particular issue must tailor the presentation appropriately.

Chapter Four

APPELLATE PROCEDURE
AND DECISIONAL PROCESSES

Although an appeal might be viewed as a continuation of the litigation begun in the trial court, it does not follow automatically; it is in form and reality a new proceeding. Like other proceedings in the Anglo-American adversarial system, appeals are party-initiated and party-propelled. A party wishing to appeal must take the appropriate steps to launch and pursue the case in the appellate court.

The procedures governing the conduct of appellate litigation are prescribed by statutory enactments and court-promulgated rules. The latter typically contain most of the details, and they must be followed meticulously by lawyers representing appellants and appellees. In the U.S. courts of appeals the applicable procedures are found in the Federal Rules of Appellate Procedure, issued by the Supreme Court pursuant to its authority under the Rules Enabling Act. They are supplemented in each court of appeals by "Local Rules." Each state appellate court operates under a similar set of rules, although the details vary from state to state.

Procedural rules of that sort have been part of the appellate world since the earliest days, governing the actions of lawyers and parties. New on the scene, in response to the late

69

twentieth-century rise in volume, is conscious attention by appellate courts to their internal decisional processes, with many of them promulgating written rules and policies describing what have come to be referred to as "internal operating procedures." These involve significant departures from traditional behind-the-scenes processes.

This chapter first outlines the traditional appellate process and then discusses the newer variations.

A. *Traditional Appellate Procedure and Decisional Processes*

Despite the rise in case volume and the changes in internal processes since the 1960s, procedural rules prescribing steps that must be taken by lawyers and litigants have not changed significantly. The sequence is as follows:

First, a party desiring to appeal from a trial court judgment or other trial court action must file a document usually called a "notice of appeal," typically a single sheet of paper setting out the name of the court and the case and stating that the party appeals from the specified trial court action. With the filing of that paper the party—now designated as the appellant—can be said to have "taken" or "filed" an appeal. Jurisdiction over the case thereby passes to the appellate court.

No response to this paper is required from the opposing party, now denominated the appellee. However, rules often allow an appellee some early moves. If, for example, the appellee wants to assert that the judgment is not appealable (*e.g.*, for lack of finality), a motion to dismiss might be filed. Also, if the appellee's position is that the appeal is clearly without merit and the court should summarily affirm, a motion to that effect might be filed. On these and all other matters of procedure it is difficult to generalize accurately across the entire American appellate domain; the rules of the particular court must be consulted.

The taking of an appeal does not ordinarily suspend the effectiveness of the judgment. If the appellant wishes to prevent enforcement of the judgment pending resolution of the appeal, the appellant must file a supersedeas bond, providing the appellee with security for later compliance with the judgment if it is affirmed, or file a motion for a stay of execution of the judgment. If a bond is filed or a stay granted, whichever the applicable law provides for, the judgment cannot be enforced until final disposition of the appeal.

The next step is the assembling and filing of the record. The appellant is responsible for seeing that this is done within the time required by the rules—typically thirty to sixty days after the filing of the notice of appeal—but most of the work is done by others. Rules prescribe the contents of the record, and they usually require that it include documents on file in the trial court clerk's office such as pleadings, motions, orders of the court, and the formal judgment. Personnel in the clerk's office will compile that material. If a transcript is needed of witness testimony or of other proceedings in the case, the court reporter must be instructed to prepare it. The appellant can request that only certain portions of the transcript be included, and the appellee can then request additional parts. The documents from the clerk's office and the court reporter's transcript constitute the record, which is transmitted to the appellate court with an official certification of authenticity from the trial court. Failure to file the record within the prescribed time is a ground for dismissal of the appeal. As pointed out in Chapter 3, this record, with minor qualifications, provides the sole basis for the appellate court's decision.

Once the record is filed, the briefing stage begins. First the appellant must file a brief within the prescribed time, usually thirty days from the date the record was filed. Then the appellee's brief in response, if any, must be filed within a stated time. A reply brief from the appellant is usually allowed.

Each of these briefs is a printed or typed document, typically a booklet (letter-size or smaller) of twenty to fifty pages, setting out the party's view of the proceedings and the facts and presenting the legal argument in support of either reversal or affirmance. Citations to all pertinent statutes and cases are included. Rules specify the precise contents of the brief and details concerning format and length. Briefs are the principal means through which the parties convey to the court their legal theories and arguments, and they are relied on heavily by appellate judges.

Courts of last resort generally permit, with leave of court, a brief to be filed by an amicus curiae (friend of the court, not a party to the case). Such briefs are typically filed only in connection with cases presenting legal issues important to certain organizations or special interests. They often provide data and arguments in addition to those contained in the parties' briefs. Amicus briefs have become more common in recent years, especially in the U.S. Supreme Court.

Traditionally, the appellate court had nothing to do with the case until the completion of the briefing stage. Rather, the process was left entirely in the hands of the parties and their lawyers. Unless a party complained to the court, there was no judicial supervision over compliance with time limits at the successive steps; the pull and haul of the adversary process was thought adequate to ensure that the appeal progressed to the point of readiness for the judges' attention. One of the changes of the last couple of decades has been the assumption by appellate courts of responsibility to ensure that appeals move along in accordance with court rules. The newly recognized premise is that the adversary process alone cannot be relied upon to protect the litigants' interest in a prompt resolution, the court's interest in avoiding a backlog, and the public's interest in efficient use of judicial resources.

After all briefs are filed, traditional practice calls for the case to be scheduled for oral argument before the judges, which usually takes place within one to three months after briefing is completed. The date is set by the court in light of its docket.

At the argument, counsel for both sides appear in the courtroom where the black-robed judges will be seated on the bench. In an intermediate court, three judges are normally present; in a court of last resort, the full court is assembled. Counsel for the appellant presents argument first, followed by counsel for the appellee. A short rebuttal by appellant's counsel may be permitted.

Over the years the time allotted each side has gradually shrunk. In the nineteenth century it was virtually unlimited, with some arguments lasting several days. In this century, courts began to limit argument to one hour per side; this was reduced to thirty minutes in many courts after the Second World War. Thirty minutes continues to be allowed in many courts of last resort, but in intermediate courts the time may be fifteen minutes or even less. Some of the most radical changes in procedure stemming from the volume crunch concern the role of oral argument, and these are discussed in the next section.

Procedures after argument vary among appellate courts. Many hold a conference in which the judges gather unto themselves in the court's private conference room to discuss the case and reach a tentative decision and a tentative line of reasoning supporting it. The case is then assigned to one of the judges to prepare a draft opinion that will be circulated to the others. In some courts case assignments are made by the judge presiding at the argument. In other courts assignments are made mechanically on a rotating basis, so the judges know before argument who will draft the opinion. One disadvantage of this practice is that it can tend to produce a one-judge opinion, instead of a genuinely collegial product, as the judges to whom the case is not assigned may rely unduly on the assigned judge and not give sufficient attention to the opinion.

Under traditional procedure an explanatory opinion is written by a judge in almost every case. It typically sets out the facts of the case, the proceedings in the lower court, and the appellate court's reasoning on each issue being decided. Each of the participating judges receives a copy of the draft and can make comments and suggestions to the author. Courts vary in the extent to which judges edit each other's work.

Either through a conference or by circulating comments, judges—at least a majority—reach agreement on an opinion. A judge in the minority may write a dissenting opinion, and a judge agreeing with the result but not with the reasoning may write a concurring opinion. Majority opinions may be "signed," meaning that the name of the writing judge appears at the beginning, or they may be designated "per curiam," with the participating judges named but no author specified. Concurring and dissenting judges are always identified. The per curiam designation may be used in relatively simple cases whose opinions inspire no pride of authorship, or sometimes in politically charged cases to avoid highlighting any one judge and to emphasize the unanimity of the decision.

State supreme court opinions are published in the official state reports. State intermediate court opinions are usually published in a separate set of books. In addition, both types of opinions are published in the regional reporters of the West Publishing Company's National Reporter System, which consists of seven series of numbered volumes. Opinions of the U.S. courts of appeals are found in the *Federal Reporter* series. The Supreme Court's opinions are officially collected in the *United States Reports* and in two unofficial series: the *Supreme Court Reporter* and the *Lawyers' Edition*. Each of these sets of reports, state and federal, consists of several hundred volumes, each containing hundreds or even thousands of pages. This vast array of published judicial opinions constitutes the case law of the United States.

Researching this mass of material is expedited by an equally vast array of privately published indexes, digests, and all sorts of secondary literature. In addition, since the late twentieth century, the texts of judicial opinions and numerous other sources of relevant information have been available through electronic database services, most notably WESTLAW and LEXIS. Such computer-assisted legal research greatly facilitates the task of locating pertinent precedents.

The opinion of an appellate court is the explanation of

what the court is deciding; it is not a legally operative instrument. The court's formal action is embodied in its "judgment," a separate document directing the disposition of the case. If the trial judgment is affirmed, nothing more is to be done except possibly the collection of court costs from the party held liable for them. If the trial judgment is reversed or modified in some way, the appellate court's judgment will order, for example, that the case be remanded to the court from which it came, and will contain appropriate instructions, *e.g.*, "that the judgment for plaintiff be set aside and a new trial be ordered." This document is sometimes referred to as the court's "mandate." .

Issuance of the opinion and mandate normally concludes proceedings in the appellate court, except that a party may petition for a rehearing. The usual ground for such a petition is that the court overlooked a crucial fact in the record or failed to take into account a relevant precedent or in some other way misconceived the case. Such petitions are frequently made by disappointed lawyers but are rarely granted. They do give the court an opportunity to reconsider what it has done and occasionally to correct a mistake. A party may also suggest an en banc rehearing if, as in the federal appellate courts, such a proceeding is authorized.

All of the steps outlined above pertain to appeals at the first appellate level, where review is pursued as a matter of right. In a two-level appellate structure, that review is usually in the intermediate court, after which further review may be sought in the court of last resort. If review at that upper level is discretionary with the court, as it typically is, the procedure falls into two stages.

In the first stage, the party dissatisfied with the intermediate court's decision seeks to demonstrate to the top court that it should review the case. This is done by filing with the court a petition for a writ of certiorari, as it is called in the U.S. Supreme Court and some state supreme courts, or a petition for leave to appeal, as it is called in others. This petition is a document, shorter than a brief on the merits, in which the petitioner attempts to show the court that the case comes within its criteria for granting review. The other party may file a statement in opposition, undertaking to show the court why it should not grant review. Theoretically, the parties at this stage should not be primarily concerned with the merits, but as a practical matter petitioning counsel almost always try to demonstrate that the court below erred. Statistics, reinforced by folklore at the bar, do suggest that a court is more likely to grant review if it believes the decision below is wrong than if it believes it to be correct.

The judges individually study the petitions and responses and then vote to grant or deny. Some courts deal with petitions in conference; others dispose of them through circulating memoranda. In the U.S. Supreme Court a petition is granted if four of the nine Justices agree on a grant. In some state supreme courts, however, a grant requires a majority vote. If the petition is denied, that is the end of the litigation. On the other hand, if the petition is granted the proceeding moves into its second stage.

In the second stage, briefs on the merits are filed by the parties and oral argument is heard by the full court, followed by a court conference and ultimately a decision through a written opinion. In other words, once a petition is granted the case moves through steps essentially like those in the traditional appellate process at the first level of review.

B.   *Departures from Traditional Processes*

The "crisis of volume" that has beset American appellate courts in the last third of the twentieth century has had a major impact on appellate structure, personnel, and process. The structural response to the volume problem has been the creation of intermediate appellate courts, discussed in Chapter 2. The personnel response has been, and continues to be, the addition of intermediate court judges, law clerks, and central staff attorneys, all discussed in Chapter 5. The process response— involving the adoption of differentiated and truncated decisional tracks—has wrought the most radical change of all. These new internal processes are described below.

Differentiated Internal Decisional Tracks

Until the late 1960s the assumption in appellate courts to which appeals came as a matter of right was that all appeals were to be treated alike. Each case would proceed through the steps in the appellate process outlined in the previous section: assembling and filing the record, briefing by the opposing lawyers, oral argument, court conference, and explanatory opinion. As dockets swelled and backlogs mounted, this assumption began to be questioned. The perception emerged that appeals did not all deserve to be dealt with in precisely the same way, that some could be fairly disposed of without the full traditional array of steps. Thus was born the idea of creating different decisional tracks, with some cases receiving more elaborate judicial attention than others. The simpler "fast track" would permit the court to decide more appeals within a shorter time and thereby avoid unacceptable backlogs.

The pioneer in this movement was the U.S. Court of Appeals for the Fifth Circuit. In 1968 it established screening panels, each consisting of three judges. When briefing had been completed in a case, the clerk's office would send the briefs and the record to one judge on a screening panel. That judge would review the papers to determine whether the case should be scheduled for oral argument. If he thought argument necessary or desirable, he would return the case to the clerk, and it would be scheduled for argument and proceed thereafter through the traditional process. If, on the other hand, the judge thought that argument would not be needed, he would write a short memorandum to that effect for the other two judges on the screening panel. If the judge thought an explanatory opinion unnecessary, applying criteria that the court had adopted in its Local Rule 21, he would so recommend. (Rule 21 [now superseded by Rule 47.6] stated that an opinion will not be written if the court finds no error of law and no basis for disturbing the trial court's factual findings and, in addition, determines that an opinion would have no precedential value.) The papers would then go to the other two judges. If either of them did not agree, the case would be returned to the clerk and set for argument. However, if they both agreed, the judgment would be affirmed without argument, conference, or opinion. The court's order would say simply, "Affirmed. See Local Rule 21."

The Fifth Circuit's screening was designed to identify uncomplicated, routine appeals that could be easily decided. That there are many such cases cannot be doubted. Over the years numerous appellate judges, both state and federal, have said that a large majority of appeals are destined to be decided only one way. If most of these can be spotted before the judges invest substantial time in them, considerable judge time can be saved and the appellate process expedited significantly.

At about the same time that the Fifth Circuit inaugurated

its screening procedure, the Michigan Court of Appeals made another kind of innovative move by establishing a central staff of attorneys. These lawyers were organized into a pool to work for the court as a whole. Although judges had had personal law clerks for years, the idea of a centralized staff was new.

The introduction of central staff attorneys in the Michigan court was not linked to any screening procedure. The staff's role was to write a memorandum on every appeal and, when the staff considered it appropriate, to draft a proposed short opinion that the judges could adopt. The case then went to a regular three-judge panel, which would hold oral argument as usual and, if it saw fit, issue the staff-drafted opinion as the opinion of the court. The staff work was believed to assist the judges in deciding appeals expeditiously because the memorandum enabled them to grasp the case more quickly and the draft opinion relieved them of the opinion writing task.

Soon thereafter the concept of screening was combined with the use of central staff attorneys by the California Court of Appeal, First Appellate District. Whereas the Michigan Court of Appeals had staff with no screening, and the Fifth Circuit had judge screening with no staff, the California court adopted staff screening along with staff memorandum writing and opinion drafting. If at the screening stage a staff attorney recommended oral argument, the case would go forthwith to a three-judge panel without any further staff work. If the staff attorney recommended no argument, both a memorandum for the judges and a short draft opinion would be prepared. The case would then go to a three-judge panel. If any judge disagreed, the case would be scheduled for argument. If the judges agreed, a letter would be sent to counsel informing them that the case would be decided without argument unless counsel requested argument. This "invited waiver" left the door open for counsel to present argument but sent a clear signal that the court did not think it desirable.

Since those early ventures into screening and the use of staff attorneys, varieties of those innovations have been widely adopted by state and federal appellate courts. Today in most intermediate courts there is early screening and routing of appeals along different decisional tracks, one track being the traditional full-scale process and the other involving, in varying degrees, bypassing oral argument, dispensing with face-to-face conferences among the judges, and using short opinions, often drafted by staff attorneys. Although procedural shortcuts could be used by an appellate court without a central staff, in most courts a staff is intimately involved with the fast-track process.

The above-described late twentieth-century innovations have caused a radical alteration in the American appellate scene. Considerable debate has surrounded each aspect of the shortened process and the use of central staff attorneys. The tenor of the controversy and the advantages and disadvantages of these innovations are suggested hereafter.

Screening

Some arrangement for threshold screening of appeals is essential to any differentiation in the steps through which judges go to dispose of their cases. In some courts screening is done by judges, and in others it is done by staff attorneys. The argument for using judges is that it keeps them more closely in charge and produces more accurate screening decisions. The argument for using staff is that it relieves the judges of this chore, leaving them with more time for substantive decision making; furthermore, the initial routing step is only tentative and can be altered later by any judge.

Whoever does the screening and whether or not the court has a staff, the screeners function according to standards fixed by the court, a feature important for heightening uniformity in screening decisions and preserving judicial control over the process. The criteria for routing a case through a truncated process and the criteria for sending a case to staff are usually the same. The wording of these criteria varies among appellate courts, but they essentially seek to identify cases that are routine and simple, involving only the application of settled legal rules to particular facts, and those in which the outcome is easily predictable. (One might reasonably ask why a lawyer would ever take such an appeal; this question of professional responsibility is discussed in Chapter 5, Section D.) The reality is that a large proportion of appeals are of this sort. This is especially true in the criminal field; most convicted defendants are indigent and are provided with free counsel and transcripts, thus removing any incentive to stop litigating.

By contrast, appeals that do not fit these criteria are those involving complicated factual situations, novel legal questions, or controversies of unusual public interest, or those in which an opinion is likely to have significant precedential value. Those appeals typically bypass staff treatment and are scheduled for oral argument.

Dispensing with Oral Argument

Oral argument was the first casualty of the volume crunch. In the move to shorten and expedite decisional time, oral hearings were seen by judges to be dispensable in many cases. The advantage of bypassing argument was not so much in saving the time the judges would devote to sitting on the bench to hear argument as it was in removing a bottleneck, permitting the case to move to disposition without having to await its turn to be scheduled for hearing amidst a crowded calendar. The premise is that in a substantial number of appeals the briefs are adequate to inform the judges of the parties' positions on the facts and the law, so that oral presentations by counsel would add nothing helpful. A reason less often articulated is that many judges have a low regard for the quality of oral argument; they think that many lawyers do a poor job and that having to listen to them is a waste of time. It is recognized, however, that oral argument is helpful and indeed necessary in some cases and that these can be identified by a carefully administered screening procedure.

Perhaps the most useful feature of a hearing is that it gives the judges an opportunity to clarify uncertainties about the facts, the law, or the parties' positions. It also affords counsel an opportunity to put across to the court the most compelling aspect of the case and to answer the judges' concerns about possible ramifications of the decision the court is being urged to make. Furthermore, oral argument makes the appellate process more visible, helping to dispel apprehensions about a faceless, bureaucratized judiciary. Judges differ in their views about the value of oral argument, some seeing more occasions than others on which it changes their minds about a case.

In the early 1970s as the move to eliminate argument in numerous appeals was spreading, practitioners became disturbed. Many believed that in every appeal of right there should be a right to oral presentation, unless waived by counsel. The American Bar Association adopted a resolution stating that belief. However, as the practice of curtailing argument spread among appellate courts across the country and as lawyers became accustomed to it, opposition subsided, probably as a result of the realization that in many cases argument was indeed unnecessary. Dispensing with argument also has the virtue of reducing the expense of an appeal, an attractive feature from at least the client's standpoint.

Today most busy intermediate courts decide a large percentage of cases without oral argument. In the federal appellate courts the percentage ranges from a low of about 25% in the Second Circuit to a high of over 70% in the Third Circuit. The figure is above 50% in eight of the thirteen circuits. In state intermediate appellate courts the percentage of argued cases is generally higher, although there are several in which fewer than half of the appeals are argued orally.

Staff Memoranda; Bypassing Conferences

The decision not to have oral argument often means that the case will be routed through the central staff, if the court has one, and will be studied by a staff lawyer who will prepare a memorandum. A staff memorandum typically summarizes the facts and the proceedings below and presents the arguments of the parties on each issue. Usually the memorandum also includes the staff attorney's recommendation of how the case should be decided. This document provides the judges with a roadmap of the appeal. It includes references to pages in the record for key facts and rulings, enabling the judges to check these matters quickly for themselves. The purpose of the memorandum is to expedite the decisional process. A memorandum also compensates for inadequate lawyering, as staff attorneys may do research beyond that contained in the briefs. This can be especially important in criminal appeals involving indigent defendants, in which legal representation is sometimes uneven.

There is always the possibility that a staff attorney may

see a case differently from the way a judge would see it. This could prove troublesome if judges rely too much on the staff memorandum. The major protection against such undue delegation of judicial duties is the judges' integrity and sense of responsibility.

Courts using staff memoranda in non-argued cases often dispense with conferences in those cases, on the premise that cases meeting the criteria for bypassing argument are also cases in which there is typically nothing to discuss. In other words, the outcome is clear, and if all three judges agree after reviewing the staff memorandum and the briefs, it is pointless to meet face-to-face to talk about it. On the other hand, there are those who think that dispensing with a conference, particularly when there was no oral argument, poses too great a threat to sound decision making that is supposed to be collegial. In some courts staff-treated, non-argument cases are listed for conference, but when the judges convene they are discussed only if a judge specifically singles them out. This procedure at least provides an occasion for discussion even if the opportunity is not exercised.

Opinions: Short and Unpublished

Cases put on the non-argument track are also cases that typically do not receive the traditional full-length explanatory opinion. Rather, they are disposed of by a short form of opinion, usually one to two pages long, drafted either by a staff attorney or by a judge. These are variously referred to as memorandum opinions or per curiams. Such opinions omit a detailed statement of facts and the proceedings below, other than in the most summary form. They simply identify the issues presented and state the court's decision, succinctly indicating the reason and usually citing the controlling authorities.

Many courts use still shorter forms of disposition like the Fifth Circuit's "Affirmed. See Local Rule 21." A one-line affirmance without explanation is known in some courts as a "judgment order" or a "PCA" (so called because it says simply, "Per Curiam. Affirmed."). Some observers believe that such unexplained dispositions undermine respect for the appellate process, leaving the losing litigant with no assurance that the court focused on the case or understood the issues. On the other hand, there are clearly meritless appeals that should never have been taken and that arguably deserve no more than passing attention from the court.

There is yet another question connected with appellate opinions: Should some of them not be published and, if so, which? Before the mid twentieth century all opinions of appellate courts were printed in bound volumes. But the rising quantity of appeals, with the increasing proportion of meritless cases, led to the perception that not every opinion contributed to the development of the law. The publication of such opinions simply cluttered the books, making research more time-consuming and expensive. Thus the concept of non-publication, which had always been accepted in England, began to gain ground in the 1970s. Non-publication policies are now in effect in most intermediate courts, state and federal.

A court with a non-publication policy usually has a rule setting out the criteria for publication. These rules generally designate for publication only those opinions that enunciate a new rule of law or modify or clarify an existing rule, resolve a conflict in the court's prior decisions, or involve a matter of substantial public interest. The idea is to identify opinions likely to have precedential value. In most instances, cases deemed suitable for disposition by memorandum opinions are also cases in which the opinions will be unpublished.

Non-publication is now widespread. In the federal appellate courts, well over 60% of all opinions are unpublished. In the Sixth Circuit they amount to nearly 80% of the court's opinions. In many state intermediate courts the percentage of unpublished opinions runs even higher. However, in courts of last resort in three-tiered judicial systems, almost all opinions are published. That is to be expected because the top court would normally not undertake to hear and decide a case unless it were one of significance to the law and thus deserved a published opinion under any standard.

A non-publication policy inevitably raises a question as to the propriety of citing unpublished opinions. The prevailing view is that such opinions should not be cited, either by the court itself or by counsel or by subordinate courts. Traditionally, one reason for this has been the problem of inequitable access to the opinions. Because printed copies are available only in the files of the court clerk's office, only those litigants conveniently located to that office and with sufficient resources to search the files could obtain them. The inequality of access is exacerbated by the ability of regular litigants, such as government law departments or large institutions, to maintain their own collections of unpublished opinions in cases to which they were parties. Another reason for a non-citation rule is that because the opinions are not destined for publication the judges may not have given as close attention to their wording as they otherwise would; hence, such opinions should not become part of the body of jurisprudence.

Although in theory an unpublished opinion should be of no use to anyone, in some quarters there is unhappiness about

non-citation rules. Situations have been encountered in which
the rule prevented counsel from calling the court's attention to
a conflict on a substantive doctrine between two of the court's
panels. Also it is argued that everything the court does becomes
part of its precedents and may contribute to the law, however
slightly or subtly, and should be citable. Furthermore, publication
is said to be an important means of holding the judges
accountable for what they do.

The now nearly universal availability of electronic legal
research services, such as WESTLAW and LEXIS, could change
the non-citation dilemma. As these services attempt to
incorporate into their databases all opinions, both published and
unpublished, the problem of unequal access is significantly
diminished.

Other Innovations
Further refinements and shortcuts have been instituted in
some courts. One example is the requirement that the appellant
file a "docketing statement" before filing a brief. The
information in this statement, including an outline of the
appellant's points, provides the court with a ready means of
checking jurisdiction and other procedural requirements; in
addition, the statement can provide a basis for the court's
determining whether further briefing is desired and whether oral
argument will be heard. This device enables the court to take
charge of the appeal at the threshold and to tailor its processes
to fit the needs of the case.

In some courts the staff attorneys' draft opinions are sent
to counsel, with an invitation to comment or to request oral
argument. Going boldly beyond that, a few courts are
experimenting with sending to counsel, in cases for which oral

argument has been requested, a draft opinion either written by or approved by the judges; early indications are that oral argument is then waived in a significant number of cases. Steps such as these may expedite the process while at the same time providing reassurance to counsel that they can communicate meaningfully with the court.

To alleviate lawyers' apprehensions about bureaucratization and to regulate their own operations, many courts have taken to publishing their internal operating procedures in booklets, similar to those containing the court's rules of appellate procedure, and making them widely available to lawyers and the public. They typically spell out in detail how the court's screening process is conducted, the various procedural routes appeals can take, the styles of opinions that are used, how staff attorneys are employed, and numerous details of the behind-the-scenes business of the court. Nothing of this sort had even been dreamed of before the rise of volume brought about the procedural innovations of the late twentieth century.

Settlement Conferences

In addition to adopting truncated procedures such as those described above, many appellate courts have been pushed by docket pressures to adopt, or at least experiment with, programs designed to dispose of appeals before they require the judges' attention. These programs were originally inspired in part by the alternative dispute resolution movement that began in the 1970s at the trial level. That movement was premised on the idea that in many cases there are methods of resolving the controversy that are more effective and less expensive than conventional litigation. At the appellate level this idea has taken the form of settlement conferences conducted in the appellate court after the appeal is taken.

A pioneer in this movement was the U.S. Court of Appeals for the Second Circuit, which began its Civil Appeals Management Plan, known as CAMP, in the 1970s. The court employed an experienced lawyer to convene and preside over conferences with the opposing lawyers in selected cases to attempt to bring them to a settlement or at least to narrow the issues. Although the value of this process has been much debated, several dozen appellate courts, state and federal, have instituted programs of this sort. Settlement conference programs go by different names, but they are often referred to generically as CAMP, after the Second Circuit program.

Appellate settlement conferences are conducted by a "conference host," who may be a retired judge or a lawyer employed by the court. The greatest success in disposing of appeals has been achieved in cases in which the only relief at stake is money damages; compromise in those cases is more likely than it is, for example, in cases involving a constitutional question or in which an injunction is sought. The dynamics of settlement differ at the appellate level from those at the pretrial stage; at the appellate stage, the facts have been determined in a trial and the parties have already invested substantial time and money in the case. Aside from that special posture, the conference is much like any mediated settlement process. In some programs the conference is not convened until all briefs have been filed, but in others it is convened at an earlier point, thus possibly saving the time and expense of the lawyers' brief writing.

Statistics show a significant number of settlements obtained through this process in some courts. An unknown factor in evaluating the efficacy of such programs, however, is the number of appeals that would have been settled in any event had there been no such program. Despite that uncertainty, many appellate judges believe that a well-designed settlement program does achieve a net saving of judicial time, although some have found such a program to be not worth the cost.

Some courts have adopted rules requiring the opposing attorneys to hold settlement discussions between themselves, without a third-party mediator, after the filing of a notice of appeal. Experiences under such a rule have not been studied sufficiently to determine its efficacy.

––––––––

Although truncated processes are now commonly employed, unease about them continues. In the view of some judges and lawyers, they present too great a risk of eroding what are thought to be essential features of a sound appellate process. Those features include an individual mastery of the case by each participating judge, a respect for the positions of the adversaries, collegial decision making, and a statement of reasons that is the product of the judges' own analysis. Others believe that all those features can be preserved through the shortened processes, assuming conscientious judges with an appropriate sense of judicial responsibility. Whatever one thinks of differentiated processes, the reality is that if they were not employed, many intermediate courts would be unable to handle their caseloads.

CHAPTER FIVE

JUDGE AND COMPANY

The nineteenth-century English law reformer Jeremy Bentham used the phrase "judge and company" to refer to the judges and advocates functioning together symbiotically in the common-law courts. The phrase is particularly apt in the American appellate realm today. Judges are, of course, the key figures in an appellate court, but they work in conjunction with and depend heavily on other legal professionals: their personal law clerks, the court's central staff attorneys, and the lawyers who present cases on behalf of litigants. This chapter describes some aspects of this cast of characters on the appellate stage, all of whom are integral to the court's decisional processes.

A.   *Appellate Judges*

The magnitude of the appellate judiciary in the United States, and its relationship to the trial bench, may be glimpsed through a few statistics. On the fifty states' courts of last resort there are a total of 340 judges. On the intermediate courts in the thirty-eight states where they exist there are 809 judges. Thus the fifty state judicial systems have a total of 1,149 appellate judges. The District of Columbia has nine, and Puerto Rico has seven. The U.S. courts of appeals have a total of 179 authorized judgeships. With the Supreme Court's nine, the Art. III federal judiciary thus has a total of 188 appellate judges. Adding all of these together produces a grand total of 1,353 judges on the state and federal appellate benches in the United States. (See Appendices A, B, and C.)

This figure does not include the judges of two Art. I federal appellate courts: the U.S. Court of Military Appeals with five and the U.S. Court of Veterans Appeals with seven. Moreover, it does not include senior and retired appellate judges who continue to sit with their courts under various part-time arrangements. If all of those are taken into account, it is probable that in the course of the year more than 1,500 judges are at work deciding cases on American appellate courts.

Even in their most expansive numbers, appellate judges are vastly outnumbered by trial judges. On the state trial courts there are some 27,000 judges. At the federal trial level there are 649 district judgeships, plus 326 bankruptcy judges and 479 full- and part-time magistrate judges, all of whom perform trial work. Nationwide the ratio of appellate to trial judges is on the order of one to twenty. The judicial pyramid narrows radically from its broad trial base up to the intermediate level and on to the single court at the apex.

Judges at the trial and appellate levels live and move in different orbits. This is contrary to the pattern in the eighteenth and nineteenth centuries when, as pointed out in Chapter 1, American judges were to a large extent viewed as fungible and served alternately on both trial and appellate levels. In that situation it was perhaps most important that a judge be one who could preside effectively over trial court proceedings, for that is what many of them spent most of their time doing. With the clear separation of function that has developed in the twentieth century, however, it has become necessary—or at least desirable—to think about the distinctive qualities required for effective appellate judging in order to choose persons best suited for that role.

Certain qualities of mind and character should, of course, be possessed by judges at any level. These include intelligence, honesty, objectivity, fair and open mindedness, and solid legal ability. In addition to those, there are particular qualifications that an ideal appellate judge should have. The list below attempts to spell these out. If not essential, all are at least highly desirable. No claim is made, however, that all American appellate judges in fact satisfy these criteria; some fine judges may satisfy few of them. The list states an ideal to be borne in mind by those who select appellate judges. This section serves also to elaborate on what appellate judges do, how they work, and who they are.

1.   *Scholarly ability and interest in the law.* Although every judge, trial and appellate, must be able to resolve legal issues, appellate judges are especially concerned with interpreting, rationalizing, applying, and shaping legal doctrine in a way that fits harmoniously into the entire jurisprudential framework. They must be able to synthesize a large and often complicated body of statutory and decisional law, identify pertinent legal precepts, analyze their applicability to the facts of particular cases, and explain the chain of reasoning leading to their decisions. Such work is quite difficult and unlikely to be well performed unless the person doing it has a strong aptitude for and intellectual interest in the law.

2.   *Good writing ability.* The written, published

opinions of appellate courts form a large and important part of the American corpus juris. They are the sources of the multitude of common-law rules and principles that govern a wide range of human activity. As binding precedents, they will be read and interpreted over the years in the attempt to apply their reasoning to the facts of other cases. The writing of clear, soundly reasoned opinions articulating the rules and the rationale behind them is at the heart of appellate judging. This remains true despite the many cases being decided by one-line affirmance orders and staff-drafted memorandum opinions, because the decisions that shape and reshape legal doctrine are embodied in full-length explanatory opinions. Even if judges use law clerks or staff attorneys to prepare initial drafts, they must still be good writers in order to edit and revise those drafts effectively; otherwise they would be guilty of undue delegation of judicial responsibility.

3. *Ability to function comfortably in a semi-monastic setting.* Although the process of hearing and deciding cases is collegial, a judge's preparation, study, and opinion writing are solitary tasks. Appellate judges work most of the time behind closed doors, on many days seeing only their law clerks and secretary and perhaps fellow judges. Persons not temperamentally suited to a secluded, scholarly existence are likely to become frustrated in the job. Political office holders, practicing lawyers, and trial judges sometimes find adjustment to the appellate environment difficult; law professors seem to have less trouble shifting from their academic surroundings to the quietude of an appellate judge's chambers.

4. *Cooperative temperament.* Appellate court decisions are group products. Each appellate judge must function collaboratively with other judges of the court. The maintenance

of what is usually called collegiality is important to the smooth
and sound functioning of the decisional process. Judge Frank
Coffin, who has often written and spoken on the subject, calls it
"judiciality" and defines it this way:

> The deliberately cultivated attitude among judges
> of equal status working in intimate, continuing,
> open, and noncompetitive relationship with each
> other, which manifests respect for the worth and
> strength of the others, restrains one's pride of self
> and authorship, makes a virtue of patience in
> understanding and of compromise on non-
> essentials, and seeks the objective of as much
> excellence in a group's decision as its combined
> talents, experience, and energy permit.

Thus to be an effective appellate judge, a person should have the
ability to work with others in arriving at decisions and
explanations that reflect a consensus. In short, an appellate judge
must be a team player, not a loner. This is not to say that the
judge should go along with a decision despite serious
disagreement. Rather, the ideal judicial temperament combines
independence of judgment with a cooperative spirit and a
willingness to respect and, if possible, accommodate the views of
others.

5.   *Broad experience in life.* Human trials and
tribulations of near infinite variety come before appellate judges.
One who has had a wide range of life experiences is more likely
than one who has led a more limited existence to understand the
full dimensions of the problems and to develop wise, workable
solutions. No particular experience is necessarily better than
another; the important ingredient is involvement in the practical
affairs of people in varied circumstances. There is tension
between this feature and the third requisite; a person who has
been active in the hurly-burly of human affairs may not also be

able to lead comfortably the semi-reclusive life of an appellate judge. However, the ideal judge would have both this background and that capability.

6.   *Wisdom and common sense.* This is related to the preceding factor but is not the same; one can have broad experience in life yet still be lacking in this regard. Wisdom can be said to be the product of experience playing upon an intelligent mind, although it involves more than simply a combination of those. It is closely connected to common sense, which seems to be an endowment that one is born with or without, although it can be honed over time. These qualities of mind are crucial for appellate judges in their unique role as both dispute resolvers and lawmakers, who sort out conflicting human concerns and articulate legal rules that govern society, often well beyond the parties to a particular case.

In this connection, age is a relevant consideration. While no bright line can be drawn, one becoming an appellate judge should have lived long enough to have gained a desirable range of experience in life and suffered some of its travails and stresses. Maturity may also heighten the likelihood of, though not guarantee, wisdom. Most people going on the appellate bench are in their forties or early fifties, and that may be the optimum age. One is then old enough to have gained an understanding of the human condition and of the legal order but young enough to anticipate a substantial number of years of active service. At the upper end, a person much beyond sixty is not an ideal prospect; there is generally not enough time left to get broken into the job and then serve a substantial period of years before retirement.

The extent to which an appellate judge should have had trial experience, either as advocate or judge, has been much debated. The argument for such experience is that appellate judges must understand trial proceedings in order to be able to review trial judges' actions intelligently; in addition, trial experience provides a basis for assessing one's professional abilities in a judicial setting. On the other hand, it is argued that other qualities are of equal or greater importance in an appellate judge and that trial experience should not be insisted upon as a sine qua non. The American Bar Association Standing Committee on Federal Judiciary, which evaluates prospective nominees for the federal bench, has modified its former requirement of trial experience with the following explanation:

> Recognizing that an appellate judge deals primarily with records, briefs, appellate advocates and colleagues (in contrast to witnesses, parties, jurors, live testimony and the theater of the courtroom), the Committee may place somewhat less emphasis on the importance of trial experience as a qualification for the appellate courts. On the other hand, although scholarly qualities are necessary for the trial courts, the Committee believes that appellate court nominees should possess an especially high degree of scholarship and academic talent and an unusual degree of overall excellence.

Unlike a trial judge, an appellate judge need not be a good manager of pre-trial proceedings or one who can deal effectively with the public or make rapid-fire evidentiary rulings and orchestrate a trial. Some excellent trial judges make poor appellate judges and vice versa. To a considerable extent, different abilities and personality traits are involved in the two positions.

Even though an appellate judge is not confronted with a trial judge's array of managerial tasks, an appellate judge should have at least a modicum of skill in managing his or her personal staff and the flow of business coming through the chambers. This has become more important in recent years because of the increase in caseloads and the growth in numbers of law clerks. To stay abreast of the work, efficiency within each judge's chambers is as necessary as efficiency in the court's overall processes.

Few if any American appellate courts consist of judges with the same kinds of backgrounds and experiences. The situation is far different in England, the mother country of the common law, where there is a single, unvarying route to the Court of Appeal: demonstrated competence as a practicing barrister, appointment as a Queen's Counsel, satisfactory service as a part-time judge on a lower trial court, and strong performance as a judge on the High Court, the major trial court. In other words, every judge on the Court of Appeal has served as a trial judge on the High Court. Moreover, every judge in the House of Lords, the highest court in the land, has been a judge on the Court of Appeal. Such a career-managed, promotional scheme is not employed in any American judicial system. Perhaps the nearest approach to it among the states was in Virginia: until very recently every member of the supreme court had previously served as a trial judge, and when an intermediate court was created in 1983 all ten of its initial judges were chosen from the trial bench. In the federal sphere, seven of the nine Justices on the Supreme Court came from the federal courts of appeals and one from a state appellate court (a degree of prior judicial experience unknown on that Court until the late twentieth century).

In sharp contrast to their English counterparts, American appellate judges have come to their positions through many routes. On courts of last resort, some judges have served on intermediate courts, but many have not. On both types of appellate courts, some judges have served at the trial level, but many have not. Some have practiced law—some in small-town firms, some in specialized work with large metropolitan firms, others in government agencies. Some have been prosecuting attorneys, some defense attorneys. Some have held elective office, often as legislators, but for some the appellate judgeship is their first public position. A few have been law professors. There is much to be said for having judges of varied backgrounds on a law-shaping appellate court, as the range of perspectives thus provided is beneficial to sound decision making.

When selecting a new judge for an appellate court, it is important to consider the professional backgrounds already represented on that court. If, for example, there were no former trial judges on the court, that would point strongly toward filling a vacancy with someone from the trial bench. If, on a court with a substantial volume of criminal appeals, there were no judge with experience in criminal matters, that would suggest that the new judge should be drawn from that field. The goal in filling vacancies should be to provide the court with a balanced membership, consisting of at least some judges with backgrounds in the major legal fields from which the court's business comes. This consideration has long been important in England, but it has been paid little attention in this country.

Given the qualities desired, or even essential, in appellate judges and the varied backgrounds from which they are drawn, it is of great importance to maintain a system for identifying persons who meet the qualifications and the court's needs. Here the American picture is mixed, bewildering, and, for the most part, sadly deficient.

The judicial selection systems employed in the United States can be grouped into four types: executive nomination with legislative confirmation, nominating commission proposals with gubernatorial appointment from the commission list, election by the legislature, and popular election by the voters.

In selecting appellate judges, four states and the federal system use the executive nomination method. Four states use the legislative election method. In seventeen states appellate judges are chosen through nominating commissions. In all other states they are chosen through election by the voters, in some on a party identification ballot and in others in a non-partisan contest.

Judicial elections have four serious drawbacks. One is that there is no way realistically that most voters can have any sense about the needs of the court or form meaningful judgments about the extent to which candidates for appellate judgeships meet the criteria discussed above—or any other pertinent criteria. Another is that a campaign for an appellate judgeship is either meaningless or improper. It is meaningless if the candidate does not explain his or her position on legal issues and makes no commitments (the correct course of action); it is improper if the candidate does promise to take certain positions, thus destroying the objectivity and independence that is essential in the judiciary. Still another problem is that when the judge is already on the court and is running for reelection, the time required to campaign, often weeks and months, deprives the court of the judge's services, a serious loss in this era of ever-growing caseloads and overburdened appellate forums.

The most serious problem relates to money. Campaigns for the bench, like campaigns generally, are expensive and becoming more so. Judicial campaigns sometimes cost several hundred thousand dollars per candidate, and candidates in some states collectively spend well over a million dollars. That money must be solicited from and contributed by firms and persons, including lawyers, who may be and frequently are involved in litigation before the court on which the judge will sit. The threat to judicial independence and objectivity is obvious, but the damage to the appearance of these essential qualities is even worse. The executive appointment and legislative election methods of judicial selection are free of the money problem, but they sometimes have unfortunate overtones of partisan politics, thus eroding public respect for the court.

To overcome all these difficulties, the nominating commission system was devised. It has been vigorously supported since 1913 by the American Judicature Society, a group of lawyers and non-lawyers dedicated to promoting the effective administration of justice. Under that system a bipartisan or non-partisan commission composed of both lawyers and non-lawyers screens and evaluates the professional and personal qualifications of prospects for a vacancy and submits to the governor a list of persons, usually three, whom the commission deems well qualified; from that list, the governor makes the appointment. Usually the appointee thereafter appears on the ballot at intervals of years in what is called a retention election. There is no opponent on the ballot; the voters are asked simply to vote "yes" or "no" on whether the judge should be retained in office. Few judges appointed under this system are not retained.

American appellate judges' terms of office vary considerably. In a few states and the federal system they hold office "during good behavior," which is to say for life, subject to removal for misconduct. In other states they hold office for terms of years and may be reelected. Terms vary from four to fifteen years. Six- and eight-year terms are common.

The heads of courts of last resort come to their positions in various ways. The Chief Justice of the U.S. Supreme Court is appointed by the President, subject to senatorial confirmation. His official title is "Chief Justice of the United States," and he is considered the head of the entire federal judiciary as well as the presiding judge and head administrator of the Supreme Court itself. In some states the chief justice of the supreme court is appointed or elected specifically to that position. In others the position rotates periodically among the judges of the court, with each taking a turn in the post for two years or so. In still other states the chief justiceship is held on the basis of seniority, with the position going to the next senior judge on the departure of the incumbent. On most intermediate courts the chief judgeship is similarly filled on the basis of seniority.

However the position is filled, the chief is considered only the first among equals. Like all other judges on the court, chief judges hear and decide cases and write opinions. In addition, however, they have substantial administrative duties. They are responsible for the proper functioning of the clerk's office, the central staff attorneys, and the court's library. It is their business to ensure that the court does not lag behind the flow of appeals and that backlogs do not develop. On supreme courts, chief justices preside at oral arguments and court conferences. On intermediate courts sitting in multiple three-judge panels, the chief judge presides over all panels on which he or she sits; on other panels, the most senior active judge presides.

In some courts of last resort and some intermediate courts, all judges have offices in the same building. That increases efficiency, as the judges can be convened or consulted readily. It also may heighten collegiality, as there is greater opportunity for the judges to see each other at lunch or in the corridors or informally in their chambers. In many appellate courts, however, the judges live and work at their home bases, instead of at the seat of the court, and are thus widely dispersed. This is the pattern in all the federal appellate courts except for the District of Columbia and Federal Circuits, which are both based in Washington, D.C. The result is that in the large circuits many judges are hundreds of miles apart, coming together in the same courthouse only once a month for a few days to hear oral arguments. The difficulties and inefficiencies of such dispersion have been lessened considerably by technological innovations. With today's telephones, fax machines, and electronic mail, memos and draft opinions can be circulated as rapidly as they could be if the judges were all in the same building, and judges can confer through conference calls without leaving their desks.

Continuing judicial education has become an important aspect of appellate judges' professional activity. The first effort was the seminar especially designed for appellate judges begun in 1956 by the Institute of Judicial Administration at the New York University Law School. In the 1960s the American Bar Association Appellate Judges Conference began offering several three-day seminars annually, open to both federal and state appellate judges but attended mainly by the latter. The Federal Judicial Center periodically provides a week-long orientation program for newly appointed judges of the U.S. courts of appeals. All of these programs typically include instruction in opinion writing, collegiality, appellate court administration, and recent developments in pertinent legal fields. These educational opportunities are especially important because the selection processes by which American appellate judges are brought on the bench contain little or no quality control and afford no guarantee as to appropriate background and training.

The most ambitious educational opportunity for appellate judges is the Graduate Program for Judges at the University of Virginia Law School. Instruction by members of the law faculty is offered in historical, jurisprudential, interdisciplinary, and comparative subjects. Each class of thirty judges attends two six-week sessions at the Law School. Judges who complete both sessions satisfactorily and who write an acceptable thesis receive from the University the degree of Master of Laws in the Judicial Process.

Apart from the substantive instruction they offer, these various educational programs afford appellate judges from all parts of the country valuable opportunities to learn from one another and to become aware of how different appellate courts function. Other such opportunities are afforded through professional organizations that meet at least annually. The American Bar Association Appellate Judges Conference consists of several hundred state and federal judges; they gather at the ABA annual meeting. The Conference of Chief Justices consists of all the state chief justices; the Council of Chief Judges of Intermediate Appellate Courts is composed of the presiding judges of the state intermediate courts. Both organizations convene annually for three-day educational sessions. Every few years the Federal Judicial Center brings together all federal appellate judges for several days of discussion about the problems of their courts. Budgets permitting, each federal circuit holds an annual conference at which judges and other court personnel gather, along with members of the bar, to discuss the circuit's functioning and ways to improve it. Some states hold periodic gatherings of their appellate judges.

B.   *Law Clerks*

A law clerk is a law-trained personal assistant to a judge. In American appellate courts, law clerks are generally recent law school graduates, usually in the upper ranks of their classes academically. They are typically appointed for one-year terms, although some serve for two years.

Credit for originating the idea of law clerks for appellate judges is usually given to Justice Horace Gray of the U.S. Supreme Court. While still a Massachusetts appellate judge, he periodically engaged a law student to assist him with secretarial and other duties. He continued the practice after moving to Washington in 1881. In 1886 Congress formally authorized such a position for each of the Justices. These assistants were then called law secretaries, suggesting, as was the case, that their duties involved a good deal of clerical, non-legal work.

In the 1920s the idea was picked up in the federal appellate courts, then in the state supreme courts soon thereafter, and, a bit later, in the state intermediate courts. Within a few years after the Second World War every appellate judge, state and federal, had a law clerk.

Originally each judge had one clerk. However, the number has increased in the late twentieth century as the volume of appeals has grown. Today, Supreme Court Justices are authorized four clerks each. Federal intermediate appellate judges may have, at their option, three clerks and two secretaries or four clerks and one secretary. On most state supreme courts the judges have two clerks each, although there are more on some courts. Most state intermediate judges have one, but some have more.

Law clerks are an integral part of their judge's daily life in chambers. They usually occupy an office immediately adjoining the judge's room. They provide whatever help the judge desires in connection with court work; the secretarial duties of earlier years are now in other hands. Clerks do legal research on issues involved in pending cases, prepare bench memos outlining the issues and arguments in cases on which the judge is to hear oral argument, and may draft opinions in cases assigned to the judge. They also edit and comment on drafts of opinions done by the judge and serve as a "sounding board," someone with whom the judge can freely discuss the cases in confidence. Because of this close working relationship these assistants are sometimes referred to as "elbow clerks."

The nature of the position means that the selection of a clerk is a personal matter for each judge. Judges vary in how they go about this and in what they look for. Many receive dozens, even hundreds, of applications from students in their second or third year of law school. Some judges review all applications and invite a few applicants for an interview. Others ask their present law clerks to screen the applications and pass along a small group of the most promising. For some judges the applicant's personality is important; for others the controlling consideration is the academic record. Some judges insist that their clerks have served during law school on the editorial board of the law review or another student-edited legal periodical. Some are interested in maintaining a geographical balance and a variety in the law schools their clerks have attended. Others employ clerks from the same school year after year. The process is quite individualized and perhaps even idiosyncratic.

Whatever the selection process and criteria, positions as law clerks for appellate judges are among the most sought after and prized of all positions available to American law school graduates. The work provides an excellent transitional experience between school and practice; it is first-rate post-graduate training in the law in operation, with a unique opportunity to observe the decisional process from the inside. Clerks often look back on their judges as important professional mentors. In some situations, clerks become part of the judge's extended family, and they hold periodic reunions.

The benefit is not all one way, however. In high-volume appellate courts, it is unlikely that a judge could keep abreast of the work without the help of one or more law clerks. In recent decades they have become integral, essential elements of the decisional process—part of "judge and company." Moreover, they are sources of fresh ideas and perspectives for the judges, and they form a link between the judiciary and legal academia. Those recent graduates coming to the judges' chambers year after year provide the judges with a conduit to the ideas fermenting among the nation's law professors and thus keep the judges in touch with emerging legal theories and proposals for law reform.

C. *Central Staff Attorneys*

Central staff attorneys are lawyers employed by an appellate court to work for the court as an entity. They provide professional assistance to the judges on pending appeals, but unlike law clerks, they have no close relationship to any particular judge. They are organized centrally under the supervision of a lawyer who is the head of the staff and who in turn is answerable to the court.

Central staff attorneys are a late twentieth-century

invention, mothered by the necessity of appellate courts' coping with radical increases in appeals. Prior to the late 1960s they were unknown in the state and federal appellate realms. As discussed in Chapter 4, the first central staff was formed in 1968 in the Michigan Court of Appeals. From there the concept spread gradually, meeting with resistance from appellate judges. Although those judges had long been accustomed to law clerks in their chambers, they were troubled by the idea of a centralized staff not under their close supervision. That arrangement smacked too much of the often maligned bureaucracy of the administrative agencies, and it seemed to suggest the possibility of unduly delegating judicial work to non-judges.

The judges' resistance was eroded by two developments. One was the Appellate Justice Project sponsored by the National Center for State Courts in the early 1970s. That project placed staff attorneys in the intermediate courts of New Jersey and Illinois and in the supreme courts of Nebraska and Virginia. Their work over a two- to three-year period was evaluated and was found, in general, to improve the courts' productivity without apparent impairment of the judicial process. That experience helped persuade other appellate courts to create similar staffs. The project also yielded the useful lesson that it was necessary to rearrange a court's internal processes to accommodate this new element, if staff assistance were to be effective.

The other development motivating courts to employ central staffs was the continuing rise in their caseloads. Each year during the 1970s brought an increase in appellate filings in many courts all across the country. At the intermediate level the addition of judges by the legislatures did not keep pace with the caseload growth, and it appeared that it never would. Thus the courts were forced to look to measures that they would have considered unacceptable a decade earlier. These included the creation of central staffs, as well as the adoption of the truncated processes described in Chapter 4. As pointed out there, these innovations of staff and process were unrelated in their origins, but they quickly became melded, the pioneer in this move being the California Court of Appeal, First District.

The American Bar Association's standards relating to appellate courts are striking evidence of the rapidity of acceptance and enlargement of the central staff idea. When those standards were first promulgated in 1977 they included an endorsement of and a short text on central staffs. In the amended version of 1985, however, central staffs were featured as more significant elements of appellate court operations, and the commentary set out a much more extensive list of possible and permissible staff tasks than was in the 1977 standards. In effect, the ABA standards provided a formal legitimation of the concept by the American legal-judicial community.

Central staff attorneys have now become a widespread and accepted part of the American appellate scene. Every U.S. court of appeals has a central staff; they range in size from eight attorneys in the First Circuit to well over thirty in the Fifth and Ninth. Most circuits have fifteen to twenty. A few state appellate courts have only one staff attorney, but most have from two to fourteen. At the upper end, the Michigan Court of Appeals (birthplace of the idea) has seventy-one and the New York Appellate Division, Second Department, has forty-three. Despite the general acceptance of central staff assistance, there are still several state supreme courts and intermediate courts without such staffs.

As appellate courts vary in their employment of

differentiated decisional processes, staff functions also vary. In some courts the staff attorneys prepare a memorandum for the judges on every appeal filed; in others the staff screens the cases and prepares memoranda only on those cases it recommends not for oral argument. In some courts the staff drafts proposed memorandum opinions that the judges can use in disposing of appeals. The twin tasks of memorandum writing and opinion drafting are probably the most frequently assigned staff responsibilities.

Among the many other duties that can be given to staff are managing panel assignments to ensure that related cases and those involving common issues get assigned to the same panel, processing applications for extraordinary writs, conducting settlement conferences, doing legal research on specific subjects at the request of the court, developing proposals for changes in the court's procedural rules, overseeing the timeliness of the filing of transcripts and briefs, and monitoring jurisdictional requirements and general compliance with the court's rules.

An appellate court with a central staff must take care to coordinate and clearly delineate the respective responsibilities of the court clerk's office, the central staff attorneys, and the judges' elbow clerks. No one way is necessarily better than another. The important point is that the court should give clear directions as to the allocation of duties to avoid overlapping work and confusion. For the understanding of all court employees, as well as for the information of the bar, the central staff's responsibilities are often spelled out in the court's internal operating procedures.

Lawyers serving on central staffs vary in their backgrounds and experiences. Some have had several years of legal work before joining the staff, and they regard the position as a career opportunity of indefinite duration. Others are immediately out of law school, like judges' elbow clerks, and they often contemplate remaining in the job for only two or three years. Views differ about which type is preferable. The experienced career attorney provides a greater measure of seasoned judgment, legal awareness, and continuity. On the other hand, that type risks becoming jaded and bored, as much of the work is repetitive; moreover, some judges are apprehensive that career attorneys may begin to exert too much influence on the judges' decisions. These risks are avoided with the recent law school graduate who is in the job for a relatively short time, although there may be a loss in knowledge and judgment. However, those shortcomings are compensated for, in the view of some, by the freshness of perspective and enthusiasm that a new attorney can bring to the work. In practice, most appellate staffs have a combination of these types, about half and half in many instances.

All agree, however, that the head of the staff should be an able, mature lawyer with substantial legal experience. That person is responsible directly to the court for the staff's performance and for administratively managing the staff, including hiring and firing its lawyers. The staff director or chief staff attorney, as this officer is usually called, is typically the only member of the staff who has contact with the court's judges, and that contact is often limited to dealings with the chief judge.

Individual staff attorneys rarely see, much less deal with, the judges of the court for which they work. Their efforts are all embodied in writing and transmitted to the judges on paper. In a few courts staff members may attend conferences with the judges to discuss certain cases on which they have worked, but this is not usual. These working arrangements sometimes pose a morale problem for the staff; the attorneys can develop a sense of isolation and of not being intimately involved with the decisional process. Unlike law clerks, they are not at a judge's elbow and thus do not experience the satisfaction that comes with this personal association. Much professional satisfaction, however, can come from central staff work if the staff is well administered and the judges take pains to let its lawyers know that they are institutionally important.

Central staff attorneys have now become so numerous and so well established as part of the appellate machinery that they have formed their own professional organization. Known as the Council of Appellate Staff Attorneys (CASA), it functions under the aegis of the American Bar Association Appellate Judges Conference, with staff support in the Conference's office in the ABA headquarters in Chicago. Through that office a periodic newsletter is distributed to the several hundred members nationwide. Members gather annually for a four-day seminar on subjects such as recent developments in various legal fields, memorandum and opinion drafting, professional ethics for judicial personnel, and the appropriate roles for staff attorneys. Speakers and discussants include law professors, appellate judges, and CASA members.

The functions of appellate courts remain basically the same as they were before the crisis of volume, but staff lawyers— now an integral part of "judge and company"—combined with the differentiated decisional processes have profoundly changed the way those functions are carried out. If practicing lawyers who left the bar in the 1960s were to return in the 1990s, they would find an appellate landscape that, though retaining familiar features, would in many respects be quite novel. Despite the legitimation and widespread acceptance of these changes, a residue of unease remains among many judges and lawyers. There are concerns that the growing judicial bureaucracy and the invisibility of the truncated decisional processes may threaten the central role of appellate judges as thinkers, deciders, and explainers. Those apprehensions are not without foundation. Yet the relentless pressure of volume leaves appellate courts little choice, given the numbers of their judges and the ways in which they are currently organized. There are, however, ideas for restructuring the intermediate tier, discussed in Chapter 6, that could strengthen the judges' role and alleviate apprehensions about undue judicial delegation.

D.   *Appellate Counsel*

Amidst all the changes in the internal appellate world, the judges remain the essential figures, helped though they are by law clerks and staff attorneys. Judges alone are ordained by law to decide whether to affirm, reverse, or modify what trial courts and administrative agencies have done. But judges act only in cases brought before them in accordance with established procedures, and those cases are brought there, in the main, by lawyers acting for litigants. Moreover, lawyers shape the cases in every way; they define the issues for decision, marshal pertinent legal authorities, and present arguments for each side. In the adversary system, which the United States shares with the rest of the common-law world, appellate counsel are key participants in the decisional process. Though formally external to the court, they are nevertheless important members, as Bentham correctly observed, of "judge and company."

In many respects the role of appellate lawyers remains essentially what it has been throughout American history. The lawyer still must counsel a party who has suffered an adverse trial court decision to determine whether an appeal should be pursued in light of the likelihood of success and the time, expense, and emotional stress that would be involved. If the party wishes to go forward with an appeal, counsel takes steps, as outlined in Chapter 4, to launch and perfect it in accordance with the appellate court's rules. However, the altered internal processes and the use of staff attorneys, resulting from caseload growth, have altered some aspects of appellate lawyering.

Lawyers today taking appeals to high-volume intermediate courts, either state or federal, employing these late twentieth-century innovations, must be aware that a sizable percentage of the cases will be routed along a fast track to decision without oral argument, a track that almost always leads to affirmance. Thus the lawyer's initial challenge—and perhaps the most critical hurdle to be surmounted—is to present the appellant's case in such a way that the screener, whether a staff attorney or a judge, will think that it deserves to be set for oral argument. In most busy intermediate courts today, a case is scheduled for an oral hearing before the judges only if the screener thinks that it contains some arguable issue of substance or, occasionally, if the case has some unusual significance attached to it. Accordingly, counsel must draft the initial submission to the appellate court—usually a brief, but sometimes a docketing statement—in a way that will persuade the screener that it presents a debatable issue, that it is not a routine or easy case. This must be done, of course, with candor, faithfulness to the record, and professionalism. If it cannot be, the appeal should not be taken. However, consistently with ethical precepts and good lawyering, creative advocacy can shape a case variously in light of the end to be achieved.

Apart from concern about avoiding the fast track, the

major difference in brief writing today, compared with earlier times, is the great importance of brevity. Briefs must now live up to their name. In the appellate pressure cooker, judges, law clerks, and staff attorneys do not have time to plow through a lengthy tome. The message must be put across within relatively few pages or it may not get across. It is essential that advocates be highly selective in the issues that they argue, and they must be succinct in laying out the argument. The brief, as always, should provide the court with the "implements of decision," in the words of Justice Oliver Wendell Holmes, by providing the pertinent statutes and cases and the line of reasoning by which the case can be decided as the lawyer urges. But today this must be done especially crisply in order to increase the likelihood that it will actually be read and assimilated by the judges.

If oral argument is held, counsel is under even more pressure to be selective and succinct. In most intermediate courts, argument is now limited to fifteen minutes per side. In some courts only ten minutes are allowed. This time stricture has radically altered the style of argument from that portrayed in John W. Davis's famous 1940 decalogue, delivered in an era when leisure prevailed in the appellate world. Although counsel still must be prepared to inform the court of the facts and the proceedings below, most courts are now of the "hot bench" variety, meaning that the judges have reviewed the briefs in advance, plus perhaps a law clerk's memorandum, and are familiar with the case. They are anxious to get right to the issues, so counsel can usually move immediately to the argument after telling the court what issues will be addressed. It is essential that counsel lead off with the strongest, most compelling point; there may be no time to deal with more than that. The Davis injunction to "go for the jugular" is the one rule in his decalogue that is now more important than ever.

With time so short, the major value of oral argument in the contemporary setting is that it affords the judges an opportunity to ask clarifying questions and the lawyers an opportunity to answer them. Skillful advocates can convey most of their planned argument by way of answering judges' questions. It is a unique moment when judges and counsel are face to face focusing on the same case; the lawyers are in effect in conference with the judges, helping them to explore the ramifications of a decision either way and to resolve their doubts. In an intermediate court with a screening procedure, or a top court with discretionary jurisdiction, the case would not be on the argument calendar if there were not some uncertainties about it. Counsel's role is to help the judges resolve those uncertainties and to do so, if possible, in a way that is favorable to counsel's client. At the same time, the occasion gives counsel a chance to put a human face on the case and to convey the equities more vividly than might be done in a brief.

In presenting appeals in intermediate courts, lawyers must be mindful that the judges function within the framework of existing law. They have little leeway in dealing with precedent. They must follow the decisions of the court of last resort and are not free to overrule or modify them. Thus, argument in those courts must be designed to fit within legal doctrine as it is. In the court of last resort, however, counsel may argue, if necessary, that a new rule be adopted or that existing decisions be modified or indeed overruled, although the latter should be asserted only as a last-ditch position. Courts normally do not like to overrule past decisions, so counsel is better advised to attempt to fit the argument into the existing body of jurisprudence, if that can be done.

When seeking to invoke the discretionary jurisdiction of

a court of last resort, succinctness in counsel's petition is of the highest importance. The U.S. Supreme Court, for example, receives some 5,000 certiorari petitions annually. Similarly, the numbers in many state supreme courts far exceed their capacity to adjudicate on the merits. Given that volume, the judges and their law clerks must necessarily skim the petitions rapidly. From twelve to fifteen pages is about all their time and attention can bear. Within that space the advocate must get across to the court that there is an important conflict of substance between decisions of the intermediate courts or that the issue presented is unsettled and of special significance to the law, jurisdiction-wide.

If the petition is granted, then the advocate's briefing job is essentially the same as briefing at the first level of review, except that, as mentioned above, counsel are less tied to existing precedents; being at the apex of the system they are freer to argue for alterations in decisional law. When discretionary review is granted, the case is almost always scheduled for oral argument because, by hypothesis, it is one of institutional importance, calling for the court's most careful attention.

Rule 3.1 of the Model Rules of Professional Conduct, in force in many states, is applicable to appellate as well as to trial work. It provides:

> A lawyer shall not bring or defend a proceeding, or assert or controvert an issue therein, unless there is a basis for doing so that is not frivolous, which includes a good faith argument for an extension, modification or reversal of existing law.

Thus, even though an irate client, having lost in the trial court, insists on appealing, the lawyer should not proceed unless this standard is satisfied.

Court-appointed counsel for indigent criminal defendants face a special problem in this regard. The Supreme Court held many years ago that the Fourteenth Amendment to the U.S. Constitution requires states to provide counsel without charge to indigent defendants at the first level of review, where appeal is a matter of right. Then in *Anders v. California* the Court held that the state had not satisfied this constitutional obligation when the appellate court permitted court-appointed counsel to withdraw after he asserted that the appeal was without merit, even though the court itself proceeded to examine the record and concluded that there was indeed no merit. This holding puts counsel in the odd and awkward position of having to pursue the briefing of an appeal in which there is nothing to argue, contrary to the normally applicable ethical standard. Moreover, the decision deprives appellate courts of the benefits of lawyers' screening of cases. The result is that intermediate courts receive large numbers of meritless—or even frivolous—criminal appeals, a major contribution to their volume problem. This circumstance underscores the courts' felt need to maintain differentiated decisional tracks.

Lawyers are generally authorized to appear in state appellate courts if they are members in good standing of the state's bar. Admission to the bar entitles one to practice in all the courts of the state, trial and appellate. However, to appear in a federal appellate court a lawyer must apply and be admitted by the court to practice there. Such admission is almost routine for any state bar member; there are no special requirements. For admission to the bar of the U.S. Supreme Court one must have been a member in good standing of a state bar for at least three years, but there are no other professional requirements.

Proposals have been advanced in recent years to require

qualifications beyond mere bar membership to practice in appellate courts. None has been adopted, and it appears doubtful that any will be. In fact, however, appellate practice is gradually becoming something of a specialty. In large government legal offices, such as the offices of state attorneys general and of United States attorneys, there are appellate sections consisting of lawyers who do nothing but appellate work. The same is true in many large metropolitan law firms. Perhaps the best known example of a specialized appellate practice is that in the office of Solicitor General of the United States, which handles all representation of the federal government in the Supreme Court.

Specialization is evidenced by the increase in continuing legal education programs on appellate practice. Intensive seminars on brief writing and oral advocacy are held at intervals by various professional groups. The appearance of a new organization, the American Academy of Appellate Lawyers, is another sign of specialization. Some law schools offer courses in appellate practice and procedure, and most, if not all, conduct appellate moot court programs. A new course at the University of Virginia Law School focuses on the structure, functions, processes, and personnel of appellate courts. However, many lawyers and appellate judges think that the law schools do not provide adequate instruction on these matters.

The rise of appellate specialization has led to a difference of view as to whether fresh counsel should be retained for an appeal. The argument for having trial counsel continue on to the appellate court is based on the reality that the lawyer who tried the case is already intimately familiar with it; new counsel would need to invest substantial time, with added expense to the client, to study the record and learn what trial counsel already knows. On the other side, the argument is that on appeal the case must be viewed through a different set of lenses, requiring a special atunement to appellate jurisdiction and practice that even the best trial lawyers may not have. Moreover, many lawyers who have tried a case are so wrapped up in the proceeding that has just concluded that they cannot readily reorient themselves to think in terms of the much narrower range of issues open for appellate consideration. There is no clear-cut answer to this question that is good for all cases. In litigation involving only modest monetary amounts it makes sense to let the lawyer who conducted the trial also handle the appeal. In a large or especially important case, however, it is usually wise for a party to engage experienced appellate counsel.

More than any other members of the legal profession, appellate counsel participate directly in the ongoing development of the law through the briefs and oral arguments that they present in the state and federal appellate courts. Those courts depend heavily on counsel and indeed could not function without them. The courts have no investigative arms to determine the facts of the cases, and they do relatively little independent legal research. Facts and law are supplied by counsel for the contending parties through the adversary process. Moreover, counsel supply the theories that feed into the court's deliberations and often find their way into the fabric of the case law. This was true centuries ago, long before the advent of law clerks and staff attorneys, and it remains true today.

CHAPTER SIX

PAST, PRESENT, AND FUTURE

American appellate courts are at an important juncture in their historical evolution. They have come to this point as the result of developments since the late 1960s, when hydraulic pressures began to be exerted upward by the rising tide of appeals. The court systems responded with changes in structure, personnel, and process: more states created intermediate courts, judges were added to existing state and federal intermediate tiers, law clerks were increased in number, central staff attorneys were installed, and differentiated internal processes were adopted.

As a result of all these changes, case dispositions have increased markedly, and in most courts backlogs have been kept under control. Judges have worked harder and have adopted more efficiency devices. But still the tide rises and the crisis of volume continues.

No diminution is expected. Indeed, more annual growth is predicted by those who have studied appellate caseloads closely. For example, federal judicial forecasters in 1990 predicted that appeals in the U.S. courts of appeals, having increased tenfold in the previous thirty years, would triple in the next quarter-century. Annual increases since that projection are at a pace that tends to validate it. Apart from their overall number, another way of

122

measuring and projecting growth in appeals is by the ratio of appeals to judgeships on the appellate court. In the California Courts of Appeal, for example, in 1960 there were 129 appeals per judge; by 1991-92 the ratio had grown to 246 per judge. The projection is that in the year 2000-01 there will be 304 per judge. Although there is wide variation geographically, nationwide the trend is remorselessly upward.

The vexing question now confronting American appellate courts concerns the steps that can be taken to enable those courts to manage in an acceptable fashion the projected increases in appeals. It is not enough simply to decide a sufficient quantity of appeals to stave off unacceptable backlogs and delays. As essential institutions in a stable legal order, appellate courts must effectively perform their functions of correcting error in lower court proceedings and attending to the ongoing, harmonious development of case law through the thoughtful, collegial work of judges.

The essential nature of appellate adjudication in the American legal order was expressed by the authors of *Justice on Appeal*, published in 1976, as "process imperatives" calling for appeals to be taken to judges who

- are impartial;
- are multi-partite;
- are identifiable, not anonymous, and not mere auxiliaries;
- think individually, but
- act collegially;
- respect the interest of adversaries in being heard, but
- inform themselves fully on the material issues, evidence, and law on which decisions are to be made; and
- announce their reasons for decisions.

In addition, the authors prescribed "systemic imperatives" requiring the appellate system as a whole to provide
- uniform and coherent enunciation and application of the law;
- decisions that are expeditious, involving as few steps as possible;
- working conditions for judges which attract lawyers of high quality, who command professional respect; and
- working conditions for judges which will foster their humane concern for individual litigants.

These process and systemic imperatives are as valid today as they were when first articulated. They are all threatened by the pressures of volume and the changes made in response to those pressures.

The threat is most acute in the intermediate courts where all appeals come as a matter of right and must be decided on their merits. In contrast, a top court with a large measure of discretionary jurisdiction can control its workload by granting review in no more cases than it can comfortably adjudicate and denying review in all others without explanation. Unfortunately, the top court's use of this device to manage its docket may cause the legal system to suffer because rising volume forces the court to review a decreasing percentage of lower court decisions, leaving more and more important legal issues without definitive resolution.

The threat to function posed by the volume crunch has been felt most acutely in the federal system. A major concern has been, and continues to be, the difficulties of maintaining a nationally uniform body of federal case law. To overcome those difficulties, ideas for restructuring the federal appellate level have been the subject of numerous studies, writings, discussions, and legislative hearings for more than two decades, but little has actually been done. To get a sense of what might be done—both in the federal system and in large state systems afflicted with similar volume problems—it is helpful to glance backward to see what has occurred since the appellate crisis of volume first began to come to national attention.

The first publicly issued warning of the rising volume of federal appeals came in *Accommodating the Workload of the United States Courts of Appeals*, a short report issued by the American Bar Foundation in 1968. Its suggestions included the creation of subject-matter courts and a national panel to resolve inter-circuit conflicts. The report's ideas were elaborated upon by its reporter, Professor Paul D. Carrington, in a major law review article entitled "Crowded Dockets and the Courts of Appeals: The Threat to the Function of Review and the National Law." Little heed was paid to those early warnings, however, and the suggested restructurings excited no interest.

Instead, attention became focused on what was perceived to be an overload on the Supreme Court resulting from a tripling of certiorari petitions within twenty years and the increasing numbers of dispositions at the federal intermediate level. To address that problem, the Study Group on the Caseload of the Supreme Court was created under the aegis of the Federal Judicial Center. Known as the Freund Committee after its chairman, Professor Paul A. Freund, the committee rendered its report in late 1972. It identified the problem as an inability of the Supreme Court to give desired time and attention to the truly important cases because of the burdens of screening several thousand certiorari petitions annually and of resolving inter-circuit conflicts. The Study Group's recommended solution was to create a National Court of Appeals, consisting of seven existing

U.S. circuit judges sitting by designation. That court would initially review all certiorari petitions, denying most of them (as the Supreme Court was doing already) and passing along several hundred annually from which the Supreme Court would select those to be heard on the merits. The new National Court would also have jurisdiction itself to decide some inter-circuit conflict cases.

Opposition to those recommendations was instantaneous and substantial. Several Justices and others denied that the Court was overworked. Strong objection was voiced to cutting the Court off from the total flow of certiorari petitions. Apparently the view was that there could be no "short-stop" in the federal appellate system, that every litigant had to have a right to knock directly on the Supreme Court's door, no matter how unlikely it was that the door would be opened. As a consequence, the Freund Committee's recommendations never had a chance of gaining acceptance.

With the Freund proposal dead, Congress moved to address the subject by creating the Commission on Revision of the Federal Court Appellate System. Known as the Hruska Commission after its chairman, Senator Roman Hruska, it shifted attention from the Supreme Court to the courts of appeals. Rather than an overload on the Supreme Court, the problem came to be seen as a lack of national appellate capacity to maintain uniformity in federal decisional law. The Commission's solution, in its 1975 report, was to increase that capacity by creating a new court to be called the National Court of Appeals, an unfortunate confusion of name with the quite different Freund Committee proposal. Unlike the court proposed by the latter, this National Court would have seven permanent judges of its own. It would have two types of jurisdiction: reference and transfer.

All certiorari petitions would continue to be filed with the Supreme Court, which would deny many, grant some and decide them itself, and refer others to the National Court. Under this reference jurisdiction, the National Court would hear and decide those cases, mainly cases of inter-circuit conflict for which the Supreme Court had no room on its docket.

Under the transfer jurisdiction, the regional courts of appeals would dispatch to the National Court cases in which there was an inter-circuit conflict or potential conflict. This proposed transfer jurisdiction encountered immediate opposition. A major argument against it was that it would deprive the Supreme Court of the control provided by its certiorari authority over when important questions of national law would be resolved.

Under both the reference and transfer jurisdictions, the National Court's decisions would be binding on all federal courts, and on state courts with respect to federal law questions, unless overturned by the Supreme Court. The Supreme Court would have certiorari jurisdiction over all of the National Court's decisions, but the assumption was that this authority would rarely be exercised.

The transfer proposal was swiftly rejected, and debate thereafter focused on the idea of a National Court with reference jurisdiction. Within a few years, however, interest faded, and that particular proposal appeared also to be dead. However, the idea of increasing the national appellate capacity by providing some sort of forum with a reference or pour-over jurisdiction to serve as an overflow chamber for the Supreme Court remained alive.

The idea resurfaced in the early 1980s when Chief Justice Warren Burger proposed the creation of a forum denominated the Inter-Circuit Tribunal that would perform the role that the Hruska Commission had proposed for its National Court; that is, it would be a judicial body to which the Supreme Court could refer cases of inter-circuit conflict for authoritative decision on the merits. The main difference between the ICT and the National Court was that the former would consist of existing circuit judges sitting by designation for staggered periods of time. Hearings on this scheme were held in Congress, but it, like its predecessor proposals, failed to gain acceptance.

Congress next addressed the problems of the federal judiciary by creating the Federal Courts Study Committee. In its report, issued in 1990, that committee devoted a substantial segment to the courts of appeals, reciting the problems resulting from the continuing and projected growth in federal appeals. Given its limited time and resources, however, the committee said that it was unable to produce a specific recommendation; instead, the report set out several proposals for restructuring the federal intermediate tier to accommodate the growth and achieve a higher degree of uniformity in decisional law. The report recommended that further study be given to these proposals.

The suggested redesigns of the intermediate level were essentially as follows:
• consolidate all the U.S. courts of appeals into a single nationwide appellate court that could sit in numerous divisions as needed and could have a national en banc panel available to maintain decisional harmony;
• create a two-level intermediate tier with numerous appellate courts of nine or ten judges each at the first level and four regional courts of seven judges each at the second level that

in their discretion would review decisions made at the first level;
   • reorganize all existing regional courts into five "jumbo circuits," thereby cutting in half the number of regional appellate courts;
   • create several subject-matter courts to assume exclusive nationwide jurisdiction over some categories of the regional courts' business, leaving the latter intact with jurisdiction over all other appeals.

These ideas, along with others, remain under study. This long-drawn-out debate concerning the federal appellate courts illustrates the difficulties of judicial reform, especially when it involves alterations in basic structure.

The creation of intermediate courts organized on a subject-matter basis holds large potential for achieving system-wide uniformity. As pointed out in Chapter 2, an appellate subject-matter court is different from a specialized court. The latter is a court that has jurisdiction only over a single, narrow category of case. A subject-matter design gives the court exclusive jurisdiction over a mixture of case categories presenting a substantial variety of legal issues. All appeals in the designated categories of cases go to that court and to no other. A subject-matter court is not "generalized," because it does not have jurisdiction over the totality of the corpus juris, but its authority over a multiplicity of case types prevents it from being specialized. The purpose of establishing a subject-matter court is to promote uniformity by making the judiciary speak with a single voice on any given subject.

The one appellate court in the federal system organized on this basis is the U.S. Court of Appeals for the Federal Circuit, discussed in Chapter 2. It is co-equal with the regional courts of appeals, but no inter-circuit conflicts can arise in the types of cases routed to the Federal Circuit because of that court's exclusive jurisdiction over them.

As the Federal Courts Study Committee suggested, additional subject-matter courts could be established in the federal intermediate tier, or other categories of cases could be added to the Federal Circuit's jurisdiction. The types of cases to be considered for such centralized appellate treatment are those in which there is a special need for national uniformity, e.g., when there is a nationwide program created by Congress and administered by a single federal agency or when the inequities resulting from divergent judicial interpretations of federal law are particularly egregious. Long-standing suggestions for such treatment include tax cases and appeals from several major administrative agencies.

The subject-matter style of organization at the intermediate level could be as useful in large state judicial systems as in the federal judiciary. Yet the concept has made little headway so far in the states. As mentioned in Chapter 2, Pennsylvania provides the best example.

Regardless of how the intermediate tier is structured, each intermediate court with a growing caseload will face intensifying problems of internal organization, personnel, and process. Once efficiency devices have been pursued to their utmost, continued increases in appeals will make inevitable the need for more personnel. This need can be satisfied either by adding judges or by adding professional assistants (law clerks or staff attorneys). If judges are continually added, thereby increasing the number of three-judge decisional units on the court, the risk of decisional disharmony also increases; the court moves closer toward becoming a Tower of Babel. On the other hand, if judges are not added, the pressure of volume will compel the court to employ more help, probably central staff attorneys rather than more law clerks (if each judge already has three or four clerks), thereby increasing the risk of undue delegation of judicial responsibilities and converting the court into something more like a bureaucratic agency.

Here is a genuine dilemma: whether judges are added or staff is added, the imperatives are threatened, yet more minds and hands are needed to do the work. How to escape this dilemma is a major question facing the American judiciary.

The dilemma results from ever-shifting three-judge panels with randomly assigned dockets. Adding judges to those musical chairs intensifies the cacophony by providing a larger array of voices speaking on the same issues. Without the additional judges, however, there is the threat of the "no-judge decision," as staff—the "invisible judiciary"—plays an ever greater role.

A large and growing intermediate appellate court can escape this dilemma by adopting a plan of internal subject-matter organization. Discussed in Chapter 2, Section B, in connection with the creation of separate courts, that style of appellate organization can also be employed by a court internally to permit it to have as many judges as necessary and at the same time heighten uniformity in its decisions and provide individualized judicial attention to the cases.

Such a plan could be designed in various ways. For example, a large appellate court—one with twenty or thirty judges or more—could organize itself into divisions of several judges each. To each division would be assigned a portion of the docket, a varied group of case categories. Appeals in those categories would be decided exclusively by that division. If there were four divisions, each would have approximately a fourth of the caseload, assigned by type of case. The court would still act through three-judge panels, but each division's panels would be constituted from the judges in that division. Judges would gradually rotate on a staggered basis, with each judge serving from three to five years in a division before moving to another. Stability and continuity would be maintained by having no more than one judge in each division rotate annually.

Several benefits would flow from this arrangement. Predictability in the law would be increased by having a known, identifiable group of decision makers remaining intact over time. If, for example, Division 1 were assigned all appeals in suits over interests in real property, from the moment a case of that type were filed in the trial court the trial judge and the lawyers would know the small group of judges from which the decision makers would come if an appeal were ultimately taken. Instead of taking a gamble by spinning the roulette wheel among two or three dozen judges, with no idea what threesome would turn up, the lawyers for losing litigants could more realistically assess the likelihood of success on appeal; the filing of hopeless appeals might thereby be reduced. Ever-rising volume could be dealt with by adding judges as needed without eroding decisional uniformity because additional subject-matter divisions could be created and the docket redistributed to accommodate the new judges. No matter how numerous the judges, uniformity would be assured because on any given type of case only a single division would speak for the court.

The subject-matter style of appellate organization is derived mainly from Germany where it is a pervasive and highly refined feature of the judiciary (although it is characteristic of European civil-law systems generally). The appellate courts in Germany are extraordinarily large by American standards. Many of the highest state courts—the *Oberlandesgerichte*—have dozens of judges. Several have more than a hundred; the average size is about eighty. Yet there is no problem of doctrinal disharmony because each court is organized internally into subject-matter divisions under a carefully designed "work distribution plan." The civil-law code system and the legal tradition associated with it probably make that concept easier to implement in Germany than in the United States. However, there appears to be no reason why the concept cannot be adapted to conditions in large American intermediate courts to preserve the imperatives of appellate justice amidst the volume crunch. The idea will likely become more attractive as appeals continue to increase, and it may turn out to be the only viable solution to the American appellate dilemma.

So-called "fourth tier" proposals to increase appellate capacity, such as that of the Hruska Commission, have focused on inserting a new court between the two appellate levels. Quite a different approach is to establish a new reviewing process between the trial courts and the intermediate courts. The basic idea is to create an "Appellate Division" of the trial courts, consisting of rotating panels of three trial judges each. At the close of a trial, prompt review would be available before one of these panels, a review devoted to the correction of error. Few opinions would be written. This would be a high-volume operation, affording every litigant one thorough review as a matter of right, with oral argument liberally available.

After a decision in the Appellate Division, further review in the intermediate court would be discretionary and only for institutional purposes. In other words, the Appellate Division would take over the present error-correcting function of the intermediate court, and the latter would then share the institutional/lawmaking role with the top court. The assumption is that the intermediate court would settle at least a sizable proportion of legal issues in a way that required no further attention at the top. Relieved of much of the current pressure, the court of last resort would then have a more manageable job of monitoring the entire corpus juris, devoting its energies more selectively to the most important legal questions. The proposal is designed to cope with both volume and uniformity, with problems of both quantity and quality.

Still another proposal advanced in response to unabated appellate growth is to make review at the first level discretionary with the court. Under this proposal, a party, instead of filing a notice of appeal, would file a petition for leave to appeal, a short paper setting out the essence of the party's contentions. On that basis, the court would either grant or deny leave. A denial would conclude the case. If leave were granted, briefs and the necessary parts of the record would be filed; oral argument would probably be heard, but not necessarily. The reason given for this procedure is that it would permit a high-volume intermediate court to dispose of many more cases more quickly. The premise, based on much experience, is that most appeals do not present any issues of real substance, or at least that the issues they do present can be decided fairly through this sort of summary scrutiny.

Opposition to this idea stems from its apparent departure from the long and widely accepted belief that every litigant should have the opportunity for one review as a matter of right. Whether the suggested procedure would actually be a departure from that notion, however, depends upon which of the two types of appellate discretion is contemplated. The two differ significantly, and it is important to distinguish between them.

One type is that exercised by the U.S. Supreme Court (the certiorari jurisdiction) and by numerous state supreme courts in states having two-level appellate structures. Those courts' concerns are with institutional review, with selecting cases for decision in relation to their importance to the law; they are not primarily concerned with correcting error in the litigants' interests. Such a court often denies review even when it thinks the decision below is incorrect.

By contrast, the other type of appellate discretion involves an assessment of the merits and is concerned with parties' interests. Examples can be found in the Virginia appellate courts, the Supreme Court of Appeals of West Virginia, and the U.S. Court of Military Appeals. Those courts examine a petition for leave to appeal to determine whether there is any arguable issue of substance; they are not primarily concerned with whether the issue is one of importance to the law. If the reviewing judges think there is an arguable error prejudicial to the petitioner, they will grant leave and receive full briefs and hear oral argument.

Another example of this type of discretionary review is in the statutes governing habeas corpus proceedings brought in the federal courts by state prisoners. A federal court of appeals has authority to review such a case only if a "certificate of probable cause" is issued by the district court or by the court of appeals. To issue this certificate, a court must determine that the case presents some arguable issue worthy of the appellate court's attention. The justification for treating habeas corpus cases differently from all other civil appeals in the federal system is twofold: a recognition that most of these cases contain no issues of substance, and the awareness that almost all of them have previously been reviewed and found without merit by the state appellate courts.

Most American judges and lawyers probably believe that the Supreme Court's certiorari type of discretion is unacceptable for the first level of appeal. It affords no meaningful evaluation of the merits, and it does not focus on whether prejudicial error has been committed. The Virginia-West Virginia type does address those matters, albeit in a shortened form if leave is denied, and that is the type of discretion the proponents of first-level discretionary review seem to have in mind. But if that is all that is envisioned, one may question what will be accomplished, other than a change in the label given to current procedures.

With screening and differentiated internal processes, busy intermediate courts are already reviewing appeals, in functional effect, in the way that the proposed discretionary review would provide. In other words, there is already a two-stage process in place. As explained in Chapter 4, the first stage involves screening, either by a single judge or by a staff attorney, and a determination of whether the case contains any issues warranting oral argument or a full opinion; if not, the appeal is disposed of by a memorandum opinion or order concurred in by three judges. In terms of depth and quality of review, that procedure, on an appeal that is theoretically of right, does not appear to differ substantially from the Virginia-West Virginia type of discretionary review.

The one practical advantage of the proposed discretionary system is that it would reduce the initial paperwork for the lawyers and would force them at an earlier point to think hard about the appellate issues; it is possible that this forced examination might eliminate some appeals. Compelling early lawyer attention to the issues, however, can be accomplished by the requirement of a threshold "docketing statement," already in use in some courts. The ultimate question is whether the appearance of justice and public acceptance of the judicial process are served better by retaining the concept that everyone has a right to one review that is not dependent on judges' discretion, even though the way in which that review is carried out today involves a large element of judicial discretion and may be much more cursory than it was a generation or two ago.

The suggestions for the use of trial judges in an appellate role and for first-level discretionary review derive from English appellate practice. There, trial judges are heavily used in criminal appeals. On each panel reviewing convictions and sentences two of the three judges are trial judges of the High Court, the same judges who spend most of their time presiding over criminal prosecutions. They are also the judges who pass on all applications for leave to appeal in England's discretionary system of criminal review.

Under that system, a trial judge (other than the one who presided at trial) examines the application, which sets out briefly the grounds for reversal (analogous to the docketing statement used in some American courts), the "summing up" of the evidence and applicable law by the judge who presided at trial (counterpart of instructions to the jury in the United States), and perhaps certain documentary evidence. The judge may obtain portions of the transcript if that is deemed desirable. On the basis of that material, the judge decides whether there is any arguable point calling for a hearing before a three-judge panel. If there is, leave is granted; if not, leave is denied. That "discretionary" scrutiny of the merits is very much like the Virginia-West Virginia type of discretionary review. It also resembles the judge-screening procedure employed in some American intermediate courts.

English criminal appeals practice is also the inspiration for another idea talked about and experimented with in American appellate courts but not yet embraced: heightened reliance on oral argument with diminished reliance on briefs. In the English Court of Appeal, Criminal Division, there are no briefs, although the judges do have a memorandum prepared by lawyers in the Criminal Appeal Office, analogous to American central staff attorneys, which summarizes the issues and the pertinent law. The only written submission by appellant's counsel is the "grounds of appeal" contained in the application for leave to appeal, conveying only a terse statement of points with citations to a few supporting authorities. The hearing gives appellant's counsel an opportunity to elaborate on the grounds, prosecuting counsel an opportunity to respond, and, perhaps most important, the judges an opportunity to explore the case with counsel until they are ready to decide it. There is no fixed time limit or set order; the judges may call first on prosecuting counsel, if that would be most useful, and they may go back and forth between counsel to sharpen the argument. The hearing is more of a conference among judges and counsel than it is an American-style appellate argument. The judges pause periodically to hold short whispered discussions among themselves. When they are satisfied, the hearing is terminated, and one of the judges orally delivers the decision and explanation.

Several experiments with this process conducted in the United States have produced generally favorable results. The benefits include the time and expense saved by lawyers' not writing briefs, a restoration of visibility and judicial accountability, and the lessening of apprehensions about delegation to staff. The immediate rendition of decisions from the bench is not a necessary feature of the procedure, but if employed it further expedites appellate disposition time.

Despite these benefits and the success of the experiments, American judges show great reluctance to move toward the English style of oral hearing with a reduced reliance on briefs. They tend to be attached to briefs, with their advantages of more carefully thought-out presentations and of portability; many also are pessimistic about the quality of oral performance that can be expected from many lawyers. However, it would not be surprising to see some American intermediate courts picking up features of the English process in the years ahead. The procedure might be especially useful in the Appellate Division type of first-level review in the hands of trial judges, described above.

Appellate argument in German courts is even more like an informal conference than the English procedure. Counsel and the judges are all seated on the same level, although at different tables. The hearing proceeds through interchanges among the three sides, much like a conference in judges' chambers. This makes much sense as a means of focusing on the heart of the case and exploring its ramifications. That sort of hearing, backed up with briefs, seems more likely to be adopted by American courts than the "briefless" English style.

Closed-circuit television could do much to restore the role of oral argument in American appellate practice. Technology now makes it feasible to link numerous distant cities so that every judge and lawyer involved in the appeal can be in a different location and yet all see and hear each other. In an appellate court whose jurisdiction spans vast territory, closed-circuit television provides a means of conducting oral argument with immense savings of travel time and expense. Some experimentation has already been carried out with this procedure, with apparently satisfactory results.

In the years ahead, the ideas sketched in this chapter, as well as other procedural and technological innovations, are likely to be experimented with and adopted (or adapted) in varying degrees by some of the most heavily burdened American appellate courts, in pursuit of two objectives: increased output of decisions and maintenance of a sound decision-making process. Although fresh ideas will appear and innovations yet unimagined will emerge, there are limits on what can be achieved through internal efficiency devices if the imperatives of appellate justice are to be preserved. Indeed, in some courts those limits have probably already been reached, if not exceeded. When an intermediate court comes to that point, it must of necessity add more judges or turn more of the decision-making process over to non-judge staff help, thus bringing the court up against the dilemma identified earlier. In the end, in order to add necessary personnel while at the same time adhering to the imperatives, some measure of appellate restructuring seems unavoidable.

Restructuring the appellate level is indeed the central challenge facing judicial architects in the late twentieth century. Ever since distinctively appellate review courts, separate from trial courts, emerged in the decades after formation of the Union, there have been only two significant appellate structural innovations in American state and federal judicial systems. The first was the creation of intermediate courts, beginning in the late nineteenth century and spreading rapidly in the second half of the twentieth. That salutary response to rising caseloads has itself now become the source of the threat to doctrinal coherence, thus setting the stage for the second innovation, the introduction of the subject-matter concept, most conspicuously evidenced in the Federal Circuit. This second innovation is still in its infancy and is not well understood. Continued caseload growth will force more attention on it, and it may be the wave of the future in large appellate systems. If the volume crunch worsens, creative minds out of necessity will doubtless adopt variations of it, along with other new structural ideas, to enable intermediate courts to absorb the number of judges they need without becoming Towers of Babel.

Whatever alterations are made in structure, personnel, and process in the years ahead to accommodate changing circumstances, it is important that the aim remain what it has been: maintenance of an effective system of appellate courts to ensure that trial courts and administrative agencies function under law. Unless the system can perform that primary mission promptly, fairly, and uniformly, the regime of law is imperiled. The extent to which this mission is performed will depend heavily, as it has in the past, on the character and ability of the men and women who serve as appellate judges. Their commitment to the disinterested application of legal precepts is what matters, even though the ways in which they go about their work may vary greatly from those of their predecessors a half-century ago. The rule of law may well be preserved or lost in the multitude of appellate judges' secluded chambers and in the solemnity of courtrooms, stretching from the Atlantic seaboard to the far Pacific, where black-robed figures sit in high-backed chairs behind a centuries-old style of bench, where Judge and Company function not only to review what happened below but also to shape the law in response to ever-changing conditions.

State Courts of Last Resort

State	Name	Judges
Alabama	Supreme Court	9
Alaska	Supreme Court	5
Arizona	Supreme Court	5
Arkansas	Supreme Court	7
California	Supreme Court	7
Colorado	Supreme Court	7
Connecticut	Supreme Court	7
Delaware	Supreme Court	5
Florida	Supreme Court	7
Georgia	Supreme Court	7
Hawaii	Supreme Court	5
Idaho	Supreme Court	5
Illinois	Supreme Court	7
Indiana	Supreme Court	5
Iowa	Supreme Court	9
Kansas	Supreme Court	7
Kentucky	Supreme Court	7
Louisiana	Supreme Court	7
Maine	Supreme Judicial Court	7
Maryland	Court of Appeals	7
Massachusetts	Supreme Judicial Court	7
Michigan	Supreme Court	7
Minnesota	Supreme Court	7
Mississippi	Supreme Court	9
Missouri	Supreme Court	7
Montana	Supreme Court	7

This table is adapted from *The Book of the States*, 1992-93 edition pp. 227-28, published by the Council of State Governments, Lexington, Kentucky.

State	Name	Judges
Nebraska	Supreme Court	7
Nevada	Supreme Court	5
New Hampshire	Supreme Court	5
New Jersey	Supreme Court	7
New Mexico	Supreme Court	5
New York	Court of Appeals	7
North Carolina	Supreme Court	7
North Dakota	Supreme Court	5
Ohio	Supreme Court	7
Oklahoma	Supreme Court	9
	Court of Criminal Appeals	5
Oregon	Supreme Court	7
Pennsylvania	Supreme Court	7
Rhode Island	Supreme Court	5
South Carolina	Supreme Court	5
South Dakota	Supreme Court	5
Tennessee	Supreme Court	5
Texas	Supreme Court	9
	Court of Criminal Appeals	9
Utah	Supreme Court	5
Vermont	Supreme Court	5
Virginia	Supreme Court	7
Washington	Supreme Court	9
West Virginia	Supreme Court of Appeals	5
Wisconsin	Supreme Court	7
Wyoming	Supreme Court	5

The court of last resort in the District of Columbia is the Court of Appeals, with nine judges. In the Commonwealth of Puerto Rico it is the Supreme Court, with seven.

State Intermediate Appellate Courts

State	Name	Judges
Alabama	Court of Criminal Appeals	5
	Court of Civil Appeals	3
Alaska	Court of Appeals	3
Arizona	Court of Appeals (2)	21
Arkansas	Court of Appeals	6
California	Court of Appeal (6)	88
Colorado	Court of Appeals	16
Connecticut	Appellate Court	9
Delaware	...	...
Florida	District Court of Appeal (5)	57
Georgia	Court of Appeals	9
Hawaii	Intermediate Court of Appeals	3
Idaho	Court of Appeals	3
Illinois	Appellate Court (5)	38
Indiana	Court of Appeals	13
Iowa	Court of Appeals	6
Kansas	Court of Appeals	10
Kentucky	Court of Appeals	14
Louisiana	Court of Appeals (5)	48
Maine	...	...
Maryland	Court of Special Appeals	13
Massachusetts	Appeals Court	14
Michigan	Court of Appeals	24
Minnesota	Court of Appeals	15
Mississippi	...	...
Missouri	Court of Appeals (3)	32
Montana	...	...

This table is adapted from *The Book of the States*, 1992-93 edition pp. 229-30, published by the Council of State Governments, Lexington, Kentucky.

For states with multiple geographically organized intermediate courts, the number of such courts is shown in parentheses.

State	Name	Judges
Nebraska	Court of Appeals	6
Nevada	...	...
New Hampshire	...	...
New Jersey	Appellate Division, Superior Court	28
New Mexico	Court of Appeals	7
New York	Appellate Division, Supreme Court (4)	47
North Carolina	Court of Appeals	12
North Dakota	*	...
Ohio	Court of Appeals (12)	59
Oklahoma	Court of Appeals	12
Oregon	Court of Appeals	10
Pennsylvania	Superior Court	15
	Commonwealth Court	9
Rhode Island	...	...
South Carolina	Court of Appeals	6
South Dakota	...	...
Tennessee	Court of Appeals	12
	Court of Criminal Appeals	9
Texas	Court of Appeals (14)	80
Utah	Court of Appeals	7
Vermont	...	...
Virginia	Court of Appeals	10
Washington	Court of Appeals	17
West Virginia	...	...
Wisconsin	Court of Appeals	13
Wyoming	...	...

---

*North Dakota statutes provide for a "temporary court of appeals," which functions only when ordered by the supreme court. It is seldom brought into existence and has no judges of its own; its three-judge panels consist of trial judges and retired judges.

Federal Appellate Courts

The city shown by each court is the location of its headquarters. Courts of appeals may also sit from time to time in other cities in their respective circuits. The states embraced by each circuit are listed below the circuit's name. Each court of appeals has jurisdiction over appeals from the federal district courts located within its circuit. This table includes all authorized judgeships pursuant to 28 U.S.C. § 44 as of December 1993.

	Judgeships
Supreme Court (Washington, D.C.)	9

Courts of Appeals

First Circuit (Boston, MA) ME, MA, NH, PR, RI	6
Second Circuit (New York, NY) CT, NY, VT	13
Third Circuit (Philadelphia, PA) DE, NJ, PA	14
Fourth Circuit (Richmond, VA) MD, NC, SC, VA, WV	15
Fifth Circuit (New Orleans, LA) LA, MS, TX	17
Sixth Circuit (Cincinnati, OH) KY, MI, OH, TN	16
Seventh Circuit (Chicago, IL) IL, IN, WI	11
Eighth Circuit (St. Louis, MO) AR, IA, MN, MO, NE, ND, SD	11
Ninth Circuit (San Francisco, CA) AK, AZ, CA, HI, ID, MT, NV, OR, WA	28

Judgeships

Courts of Appeals

Tenth Circuit (Denver, CO) CO, KS, NM, OK, UT, WY	12
Eleventh Circuit (Atlanta, GA) AL, FL, GA	12
District of Columbia Circuit (Washington, D.C.) DC	12
Federal Circuit (Washington, D.C.) jurisdiction not limited territorially	12

In addition to the above Article III courts, there are two Article I appellate courts: the Court of Veterans Appeals, with seven judges, and the Court of Military Appeals, with five. Both are based in Washington, D.C.

Selected Writings and Other Sources

Books about American appellate courts—their structure, organization, processes, and personnel—include the following:

Aldisert, Ruggero J., *Opinion Writing* (West Publishing Co., 1990).

American Bar Association, *Standards Relating to Appellate Courts* (1977, revised version projected for 1994).

Carrington, Paul D. & Daniel J. Meador, Maurice Rosenberg, *Justice on Appeal* (West Publishing Co., 1976).

Coffin, Frank M., *The Ways of a Judge* (Houghton Mifflin, 1980).

Leflar, Robert A., *Appellate Judicial Opinions* (West Publishing Co., 1974).

_____, *Internal Operating Procedures of Appellate Courts* (American Bar Foundation, 1976).

Llewellyn, Karl N., *The Common Law Tradition: Deciding Appeals* (Little, Brown, 1960).

Martineau, Robert J., *Modern Appellate Practice: Federal and State Civil Appeals* (The Lawyers Co-operative Publishing Co./Bancroft-Whitney Co., 1983) (with 1993 Supplement).

Marvell, Thomas B., *Appellate Courts and Lawyers*, (Greenwood Press, 1978).

Meador, Daniel J., *Appellate Courts: Staff and Process in the Crisis of Volume* (West Publishing Co., 1974).

Rubin, Alvin B. & Laura B. Bartell, *Law Clerk Handbook* (Federal Judicial Center, 1989).

Stern, Robert L., *Appellate Practice in the United States*, 2d ed. (Bureau of National Affairs, 1989).

Stern, Robert L. & Eugene Gressman, Stephen M. Shapiro, Kenneth S. Geller, *Supreme Court Practice*, 7th ed. (Bureau of National Affairs, 1993).

Books dealing with appellate advocacy in the contemporary setting include the following:

Aldisert, Ruggero J., *Winning on Appeal* (Clark Boardman Callaghan, 1992).

American Bar Association, Section on Litigation, *Appellate Practice Manual* (Priscilla Anne Schwab ed., 1992).

Fontham, Michael, *Written and Oral Advocacy* (Wiley Law Publications, 1985).

The following organizations are variously involved with appellate courts and their work through research, educational programs for appellate judges, or technical assistance or funding in support of appellate courts.

American Judicature Society
25 E. Washington
Suite 1600
Chicago, IL 60602

Appellate Judges Conference
American Bar Association
750 North Lake Shore Drive, 10th Floor
Chicago, IL 60611

Federal Judicial Center
One Columbus Circle, N.E.
Washington, DC 20002

National Center for State Courts
300 Newport Avenue
Williamsburg, VA 23187-8798

State Justice Institute
1650 King Street
Alexandria, VA 22314

Apart from the Appellate Judges Conference of the American Bar Association, the two national organizations concerned exclusively with appellate courts are the Conference of Chief Justices and the Council of Chief Judges of Intermediate Appellate Courts. The secretariat for both is the National Center for State Courts, at the address shown above.

INDEX

151

About the Authors . . .

DANIEL JOHN MEADOR is the James Monroe Professor of Law at the University of Virginia. His teaching and research interests have centered on the courts and their processes in the United States, as well as in England and Germany.

He served as Director of the Appellate Justice Project of the National Center for State Courts (1972-74) and as Vice Chairman of the American Bar Association's Action Commission to Reduce Court Costs and Delay (1979-84). He was a member of the Advisory Council on Appellate Justice (1971-75), the Council on the Role of Courts (1979-83), and the Board of Directors of the State Justice Institute (1986-92). From 1977 to 1979 he was Assistant Attorney General in charge of the Office for Improvements in the Administration of Justice in the United States Department of Justice. In addition to his teaching responsibilities, he has served as Director of the Graduate Program for Judges at the University of Virginia School of Law since 1979.

JORDANA SIMONE BERNSTEIN is a member of The Florida Bar. She received an A.B. from Harvard and Radcliffe in 1989 and a J.D. from the University of Virginia in 1992. During law school she assisted Professor Meador with *American Courts*, the development of material for a new course on appellate courts, and other related projects.

She served as law clerk to Judge Paul H. Roney of the United States Court of Appeals for the Eleventh Circuit (1992-93) and is currently clerking for Judge Martha C. Warner of Florida's Fourth District Court of Appeal.